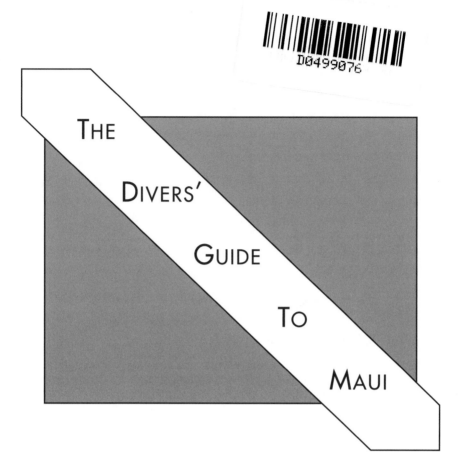

THE
DIVERS'
GUIDE
TO
MAUI

CHUCK THORNE

Author's Note

This guide attempts to provide average ratings of difficulty based upon the author's experience. Hawaiian waters change with little notice and surface and subsurface conditions may become very rough; hence, entry and exit from even the easiest rated dive can be extremely hazardous for the most experienced of divers. It is recommended to always dive with a person familiar with local waters.

At the time of this writing, all of the locations described in this book are open for public use by the various land owners. However, land ownership often changes and sites open to the public today may not be tomorrow. The author encourages that permission be obtained to cross private property where required, and that fences, locked gates, livestock, and private drives be respected at all times.

Additional copies of this book may be obtained by writing to:
Maui Dive Guide
P. O. Box 40
Hana, HI 96713

Written and researched by: Chuck Thorne
Black and white photographs by: Chuck Thorne
Cover photo by: Chuck Thorne
Book Design, Layout and Map Work by: Heather Young
Courtesy of Beyond Graphics

TABLE OF CONTENTS

Before You Dive

The purpose of this book is not to outline each and every area on the island which can be construed as a dive site, but rather, to assemble a collection of dive sites representative of a full spectrum of diving abilities. I have also attempted to divulge dive sites not only advantageous to visitors on Maui, but to kamaainas as well. Finally, I've tried to include spots on all sides of the island; not only in heavily populated tourist areas. All sites are accessible without the use of a boat, with the obvious exception of Molokini Crater.

On the inside front cover map of the island of Maui, I've started with Honolua Bay, one of Maui's most popular and colorful beginner dive and snorkel spots, and continued counter-clockwise around the island listing dive sites along the way. Since Maui's west shore is the most protected from rough seas and high winds, you'll find the safest diving on this side of the island and early in the book. The south, east and north shores of the island generally consist of more difficult dives due to the rougher sea conditions and are delineated later in the book.

I've described "Skill Levels" with three simple gradations:

BEGINNER: Divers fresh out of certification class. Snorkelers just learning how not to drink salt water.

INTERMEDIATE: Divers comfortable with the use of their equipment and having made a couple dozen dives on their own. Snorkelers good at "free diving."

ADVANCED: Divers in good physical condition, owning their own gear, strong swimmers, skilled in rough water entries, and having knowledge of currents and tides in Hawaiian waters. Generally, those with over 100 logged dives and possibly cave diving certification.

In case you hope to bring home dinner, consult your local dive shop personnel to find out which fish are edible and preferable. Also which are poisonous! DO NOT spear anything unless you know what it is beforehand. There are several good books on the subject of Hawaiian fishes available locally. The most complete is *Fishes of Hawaii*, by Spencer Wilkie Tinker.

One final note: Above all...TAKE HOME YOUR TRASH. And don't be afraid to take home a piece or two of somebody else's! Also, please don't jump in and dive where fishermen are fishing already; they were there first. Show them the courtesy they deserve.

Using this book as a guide, you'll be able to experience dive sites previously unheard of by visitors to Maui. Don't abuse it. DIVE SAFELY!

Chuck Thorne

In Case of Emergency

FIRE 911

AMBULANCE 911

POLICE 911

MAUI MEMORIAL HOSPITAL 244-2404
   This is the number for the hyperbaric chamber on Maui.
   It's only a single chamber suitable for minor recompression.

HONOLULU RESCUE CONTROL CENTER
   (on Oahu) . . . . (1-808)546-7109

COAST GUARD (on Maui) 244-5256

HANA MEDICAL CENTER 248-8294

Weather Information

RECORDED FORECASTS
   *Marine 877-3477
   Island of Maui 877-5111
   Maui Recreational 871-5054

OTHER WEATHER INFORMATION 877-6825

Other Numbers of Interest

DEPT. OF LAND AND NATURAL RESOURCES 871-4315

DIVISION OF CONSERVATION AND RESOURCES 244-4414

WILDLIFE BIOLOGIST 244-4352

DIVISION OF AQUATIC RESOURCES 244-2072

DIVISION OF STATE PARKS
   Camping and Cabin Reservations 243-5354
   Waianapanapa Park Caretaker 248-8061

HARBORS DIVISION
   Lahaina 661-3557
   Maalaea 244-7041
   Harbor Master & Pilot (Kahului) 877-6051

---

* The Marine recorded weather forecast is of particular interest to divers heading to the north, south and
   east Maui sites. Listen carefully to the height of the seas and also to the wind direction and velocity.

DEPARTMENT OF LAND AND NATURAL RESOURCES

Division of Conservation and Resources Enforcement

SEASONS, SIZES, BAG LIMITS, AND OTHER RESTRICTIONS ON THE TAKING OF SHELLFISH, CRUSTACEANS AND MOLLUSKS

SPECIES	OPEN SEASON	BAG LIMIT	MINIMUM SIZE		OTHER RESTRICTIONS
			Home Consumption	Sale	Use of explosives, electrofishing devices, firearms or poisonous substances is unlawful.
Spiny Lobster	Sept. - Apr. HRS 188-57	none	31/4 inch carapace lenth LNR 13-89-1		The spearing of any Spiny Lobster, Slipper Lobster, Samoan Crab, Kuahonu Crab or Kona Crab is prohibited. HRS 188-25 LNR 13-47-2
Slipper Lobster	Sept. - Apr. HRS 188-57	none	none	1 pound HRS 188-40	
Samoan Crab	all year	none (Hilo Bay: 3 crabs) LNR 13-47-2	6 inches across the back LNR 13-84-1		The taking or possession of any Spiny Lobster, Slipper Lobster, Samoan Crab, Kuahonu Crab, or Kona Crab with eggs is prohibited. HRS 188-58 LNR 13-84-1 LNR 13-47-2
Kona Crab	Sept. - Apr. HRS 188-57	none	none	4 inch length or width of back. HRS 188-40	
Kuahonu (White) Crab	all year	none	none	4 inch length or width of back. HRS 188-40	Hilo Bay: no more than 5 crabs nets per fisherman. LNR 13-47-2
Opihi	all year	none	11/4 inch shell or 1/2 inch meat diameter LNR 13-92-1		Any Opihi jewelry shells must measure 11/4 inch in diameter. LNR 13-92-1
Clam	7am first Monday of Sept. - Oct. 31 LNR 13-85-2	1 gallon with shell on. LNR 13-85-2	1 inch across widest part of shell LNR 13-85-2	11/2 inch measured the long way. HRS 188-40	SEASON SUSPENDED STATE WIDE UNITL FURTHER NOTICE. LNR 13-85-2
Pearl, Coral Rock, Eastern and Japanese Oyster, Top-shell Quahog, Clam and Abalone	NO OPEN SEASON LNR 13-83-1				Taking or selling any of these shellfish is by permit only. LNR 13-83-2
Octopus (day and night squid)	all year	none	1 pound in weight LNR 13-86-1	1 pound in weight HRS 188-40	none

note: "HRS" indicates the Hawaii Revised Statutes; "LNR" indicates Administrative Rules of the Department of Land and Natural Resources, Title 13.

THE INFORMATION ON THIS PUBLICATION IS AN ABSTRACT OF THE APPLICABLE LAWS AND RULES. FULL COPIES OF THESE LAWS AND RULES ARE AVAILABLE FOR INSPECTION AT ANY OFFICE OF THE DEPARTMENT, OR PUBLIC LIBRARIES.

FOR MORE INFORMATION, OR TO REPORT SUSPECTED VIOLATIONS, CALL THE CONSERVATION HOTLINE 548-5918 (Oahu)
Neighbor Islands, Call toll free Enterprise Operator 5469

Division of Conservation and Resources Enforcement

SEASONS, SIZES, BAG LIMITS, AND OTHER RESTRICTIONS ON THE TAKING OF FISH FROM HAWAIIAN WATERS

SPECIES	OPEN SEASON	BAG LIMIT	MINIMUM SIZE — Home Consumption	MINIMUM SIZE — Sale	OTHER RESTRICTIONS (Use of explosives, electrofishing devices, firearms or poisonous substances is unlawful.)
Aholehole and Manini	all year	none (Waikea Pond, Hilo: 20 per day in combination) LNR 13-63-3	none	5 inches HRS 188-40	No spearing less than 5 inches. HRS 188-25
Weke, Moana, Kumu	all year	none	none	7 inches HRS 188-40	No spearing less than 7 inches. HRS 188-25
Awa, Oio, Kala and Opelu Kala	all year	none 3 crabs)	none	9 inches HRS 188-25	No spearing less than 9 inches. HRS 188-25
Opakapaka, Uku Ula ula and Uhu	all year	none	none	1 pound HRS 188-40	No spearing less than 1 pound. HRS 188-25
Mullet - Ama'ama	March - Nov.	none (Hilo Bay: 20 per day in combination) LNR 13-47-2 (Waiakea Bay, Hilo: limit of 10) LNR 13-63-3	none	7 inches HRS 188-40	No spearing less than 7 inches. HRS 188-25
Moi	all year	15 per day LNR 13-88-1	none	7 inches HRS 188-40	Fish dealers and peddlers may possess more than 15 moi. LNR 13-88-1
Moi-li'i and Oama	all year	50 per day each species. LNR 13-88-1	none	not for sale HRS 188-40	No spearing of either species. HRS 188-25 (Moi-li'i & Oama are Moi & Weke less than 7 inches in length)
Ulua, Papio, Omilu	all year	20 in combination LNR 13-87-1	7 inches LNR 13-87-1	1 pound HRS 188-40	No spearing less than 1 pound. HRS 188-25 (Restrictions do not apply to Omaka)
Nehu	all year	1 gallon per day LNR 13-90-1	none	not for sale HRS 188-40	Nets for taking Nehu for home consumption are not to exceed 50 feet in length. LNR 13-90-1
Akule	all year	none	none	none	Net mesh not less than 1½ inches. HRS 188-29
Halalu, Hahalalu	all year	none	none	none	No netting permitted July - October. HRS 188-29
Opelu	all year	none	none	none	Unlawful to use fish or animal bait except with hook and line in the waters of So. Kona, Island of Hawaii. HRS 188-46
Sea Turtles	FEDERAL AND STATE LAWS PROHIBIT THE TAKING OF ALL SEA TURTLES.				

note: "HRS" indicates the Hawaii Revised Statutes; "LNR" indicates Administrative Rules of the Department of Land and Natural Resources, Title 13.

THE INFORMATION ON THIS PUBLICATION IS AN ABSTRACT OF THE APPLICABLE LAWS AND RULES. FULL COPIES OF THESE LAWS AND RULES ARE AVAILABLE FOR INSPECTION AT ANY OFFICE OF THE DEPARTMENT, OR PUBLIC LIBRARIES.

FOR MORE INFORMATION, OR TO REPORT SUSPECTED VIOLATIONS, CALL THE CONSERVATION HOTLINE 548-5918 (Oahu)
Neighbor Islands, Call toll free Enterprise Operator 5469

HONOLUA BAY

ACTIVITY   SCUBA or Snorkel

SKILL LEVEL   Beginner to Intermediate Divers and Snorkelers

DEPTH   35 Feet is about the maximum

TRANSPORTATION   Car

DIRECTIONS   Coming from Lahaina: Travel north on the Honoapiilani Highway approximately 7 1/2 miles past the main entrance to Kaanapali. This is 6/10 mile past the 32 mile marker or approximate 1/2 mile past Makuleia Bay. Park at the bottom of the hill on your left. This is just before the road makes a sharp turn to the left. Walk in on the dirt road to the old boat ramp. The road is too rough and often muddy to drive in any further.

WHEN   Generally, it's calmest during the SUMMER.

WHERE TO DIVE   Divers should head out to the right (north end of the bay) for deeper water. Snorkelers can find shallower water and a few arches in the twenty foot deep range (just deep enough to go down, swim through and test their breath-hold ability) on the left side of the bay.

WHAT TO EXPECT   Beautiful reef to both the left and right side of the bay. A narrow black sand beach for sun bathing. All in all, it's a beautifully protected bay with a good variety of typical reef fish to check out. No spearing, however, it's a game preserve.

HAZARDS   Winter's northwest swell can be a major problem and preclude diving activities entirely. Look out for boat traffic during the summer.

FACILITIES   None.

COMMENTS   The entry from the black sand beach is a simple matter. No wet suit is needed for protection. Remember, Honolua Bay and Makuleia over to the left (south) are both natural area preserves. No shelling, fishing, etc.

Honolua Bay

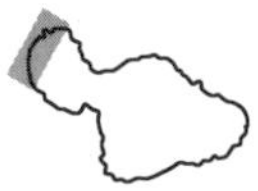

Overlooking
Honolua Bay.

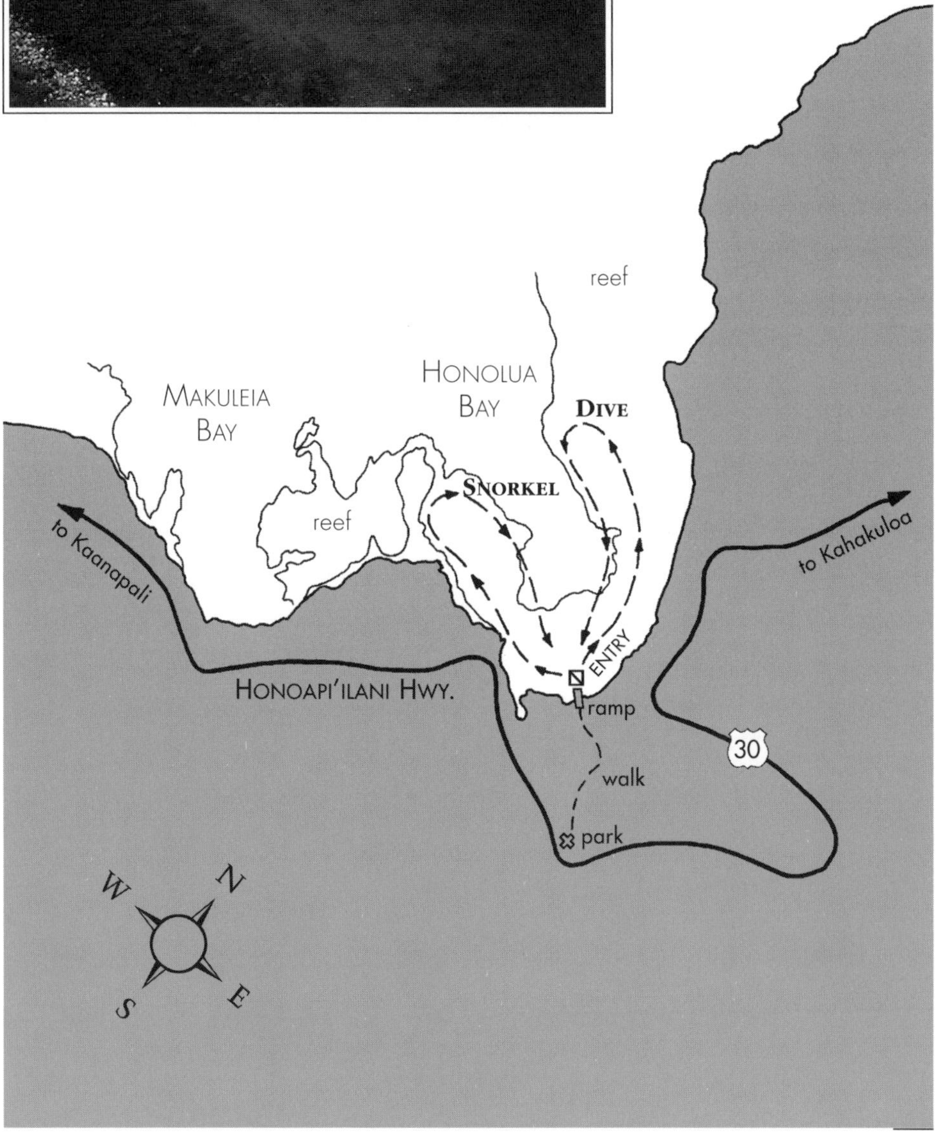

reef

MAKULEIA
BAY

HONOLUA
BAY

DIVE

SNORKEL

reef

to Kaanapali

to Kahakuloa

HONOAPI'ILANI HWY.

ENTRY

ramp

30

walk

park

W N E S

Makuleia Bay (Slaughterhouse)

Activity	SCUBA or Snorkel
Skill Level	Beginner to Intermediate Level Divers and Snorkelers
Depth	40 feet maximum on either side
Transportation	Car
Directions	Coming from Lahaina: Travel north on the Honoapiilani Highway. 6.9 miles past the main entrance to Kaanapali and just past the 32 mile marker, look for a small dirt strip on the ocean side of the road. You can park here. There are two trails down, one to the right for snorkeling and the beach, and one almost right in front of the parking area which leads down the lava flow on the left.
When	SUMMER is best. This bay is famous for body-surfing in the winter.
Where to Dive	Snorkel out around the point on the right for a short ways and then double back. SCUBA divers should head straight out from the point on the left of the bay, bearing slightly to their left. The entry/exit is well protected on the south side of the lava rock finger.
What to Expect	The reef area on the left side is really colorful and fairly irregular in shape providing good habitat for marine life. The reef turns into sand bottom at the 45 ft. depth. Snorkelers and divers both will enjoy this side. Snorkeling is also good on the right but it's not quite deep enough to warrant a tank.
Hazards	Be careful of the steep walk down with heavy SCUBA gear on. Also, watch out for the northwest swell during the winter months.
Facilities	Only the lunch wagon that sometimes parks at the top of the hill and peddles his wares.
Comments	Makuleia Bay is another MARINE AREA PRESERVE.

MAKULEIA BAY (Slaughterhouse)

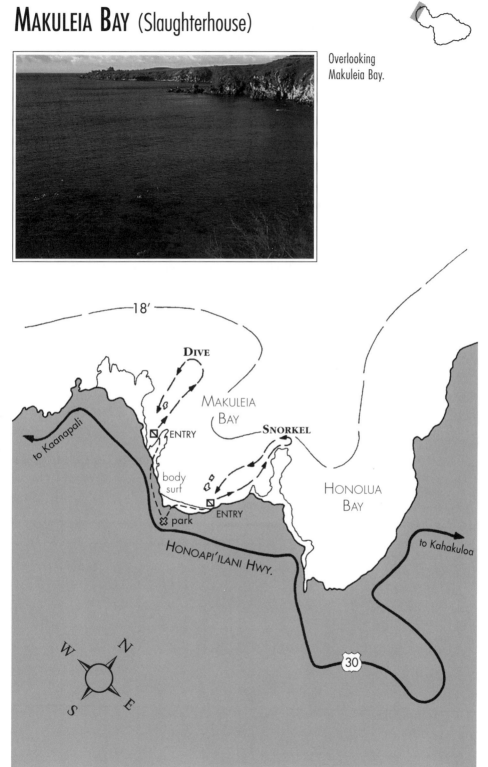

Overlooking
Makuleia Bay.

18'

DIVE

MAKULEIA
BAY

SNORKEL

ENTRY

to Kaanapali

body
surf

ENTRY

park

HONOLUA
BAY

HONOAPI'ILANI HWY.

to Kahakuloa

30

N
W   E
S

Kapalua Bay

ACTIVITY   SCUBA or Snorkel

SKILL LEVEL   Beginner Divers/Intermediate Level Snorkelers

DEPTH   45 feet maximum

TRANSPORTATION   Car

DIRECTIONS   Coming from Lahaina: Travel north 5 1/2 miles past the main entrance to Kaanapali. Turn left at the sign for Kapalua onto Office Road. Follow this down to the end and turn left again onto the Lower Honoapiilani Road. Go 7/10 mile to the entrance for the Napili Lani (You will pass the Kapalua Hotel entrance and Bay Club). Turn right and look for a small public parking lot, shower, and a walking tunnel heading north to the beach.

WHEN   Best in the SUMMER.

WHERE TO DIVE   Straight out in front of the lava flow bearing a little to the left. Follow the reef.

WHAT TO EXPECT   A good size reef with plenty of good relief. Also a good population of typical reef fish.

HAZARDS   An occasional strong current running to the right and some heavy boat traffic in the summer. Also, heads up for wind surfers.

FACILITIES   Parking, showers, restroom, and beach concessions.

COMMENTS   Kapalua Bay is fronted by a really beautiful sand beach. It's a nice place to relax and warm up after the dive.

The protected waters of Kapalua Bay.

Kapalua Bay

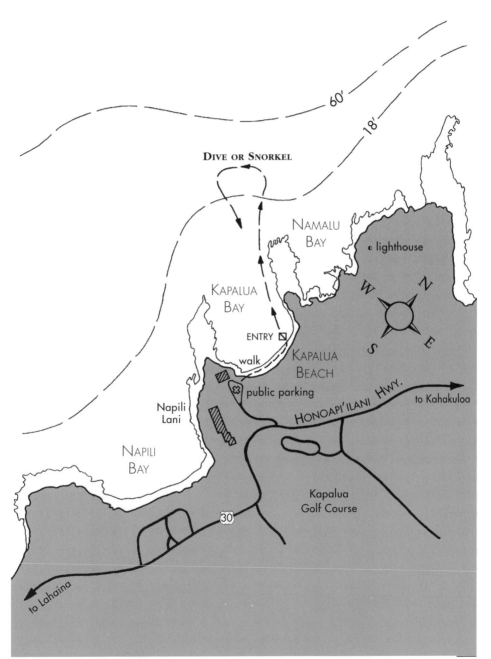

60'

18'

Dive or Snorkel

Namalu Bay

• lighthouse

Kapalua Bay

W N

ENTRY ▣

S E

walk

Kapalua Beach

Honoapi'ilani Hwy.

to Kahakuloa

✚ public parking

Napili Lani

Napili Bay

Kapalua Golf Course

30

to Lahaina

BLACK ROCK (The Sheraton)

ACTIVITY	Snorkel mainly; SCUBA for beginners
SKILL LEVEL	Beginner Snorkelers and Divers
DEPTH	20 feet
TRANSPORTATION	Car
DIRECTIONS	If you can find Kaanapali, you can find the Sheraton.
WHEN	YEAR-ROUND, but best in SUMMER.
WHERE TO DIVE	Enter at Hanakaoo Beach at the south side of the hotel and swim around the rock wall to the north and Kaanapali Beach. Concentrate mainly close to the wall for the highest concentration of marine life.
WHAT TO EXPECT	An AMAZING number of fish species frequent the area, probably due to people feeding the fish. Some observed species include: UHU, TRUMPET FISH, NEEDLE FISH, WEKE, OMILU, LEMON SPOT AND YELLOW STRIPED OMILU, UNICORN FISH, PALANI, PUALU, SERGEANT MAJORS, HUMUHUMUNUKUNUKUAPUA'A, MOI, AKULE, SADDLEBACK WRASSE, DAMSEL FISH, LEMON BUTTERFLY FISH, CHRISTMAS WRASSE and others. GREEN SEA TURTLES and EAGLE RAYS may also be present.
HAZARDS	Bumping into other divers!
FACILITIES	Only the hotel's.
COMMENTS	The entry is easy and the beach is terrific. This is also a great spot for a beginner night dive: just follow the wall down and back. Finally, please refrain from feeding the fish. This may attract fish to the site just as bears are attracted to a garbage dump, but in both cases it lessens the animals' ability to forage normally in their natural environment.

Enter from here.

BLACK ROCK (The Sheraton)

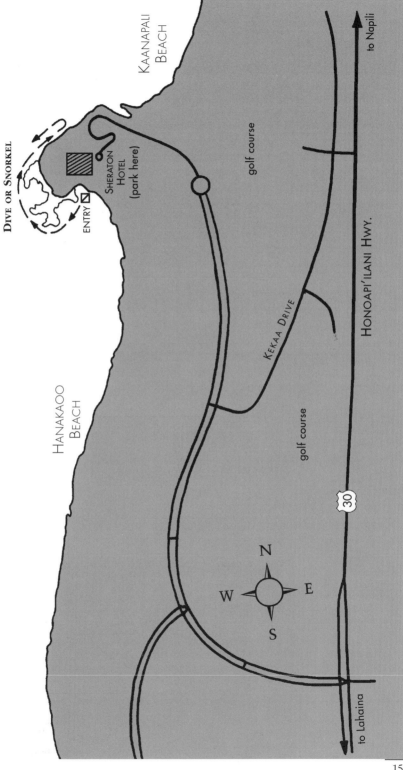

DIVE OR SNORKEL

ENTRY

SHERATON HOTEL (park here)

KAANAPALI BEACH

HANAKAOO BEACH

golf course

golf course

KEKAA DRIVE

HONOAPI'ILANI HWY.

30

to Napili

to Lahaina

N
W   E
S

OLOWALU

ACTIVITY Snorkel mostly; SCUBA if you're going out deep or you're not too good at free diving.

SKILL LEVEL Beginners at SCUBA or Snorkeling are sure to like this spot. There's a lot to see and not much to hurt you.

DEPTH A maximum of 30 to 35 feet where the reef runs out

TRANSPORTATION Car

DIRECTIONS Going south from Lahaina, pass the Olowalu General Store by about one mile and look to the right. Almost anywhere along here is fine.

WHEN YEAR-ROUND but best in the SUMMER.

WHERE TO DIVE Almost anywhere. The further out you go, the more fish you're likely to see.

WHAT TO EXPECT An extensive and colorful reef. Coral heads reach up to just below the surface of the water throughout the area and can be dangerous in periods of even moderate swells. Several varieties of REEF FISH, EELS, RAYS, and TURTLES can be found.

HAZARDS Winter's northwest swell and periods of swells from the south can pump surf in here, thereby making the diving nasty.

FACILITIES Not a thing.

COMMENTS Here's probably one of the foremost beginner snorkel spots on the island. If you're new to the sport, don't pass this one up.

OLOWALU

to Kahului/Kihei

30

HIGHWAY

HONOAPI'ILANI

ENTRY

OLOWALU BEACH

ENTRY

SNORKEL

to Lahaina

HEKILI POINT

Scenic Lookout

Activity	SCUBA
Skill Level	Intermediate Level Divers
Depth	30 to 40 feet on the left; 60 feet on the right
Transportation	Car
Directions	Look for the signs half way between Olowalu and Maalaea. It's easy to spot (8.5 mile marker approximately). Park near the center of the handrail and walk straight down to the ocean on the poor excuse for a trail.
When	YEAR-ROUND.
Where to Dive	Go left or right. The terrain is more irregular and seems to support more marine life over on the right.
What to Expect	A really nice dive centrally located between Kihei and Lahaina. Probably the best in the area. The trail down is a little steep, but it's well worth it. You'll see plenty of fish, including UHU, PALANI, NENUE, UKU, PAPIO, TRUMPET FISH, and even an occasional gray REEF SHARK (well, you may not, but I have).
Hazards	The trail down is a bit slippery and the entry can be treacherous if the water is rough.
Facilities	Typically, zero.
Comments	Here's another excellent spot for a night dive. This time, follow the wall to the west and then double back to your exit. Be sure to mark the lava rock entry with a shore light to guide the way back. Remember not to leave anything valuable in your car.

Enter here.

SCENIC LOOKOUT

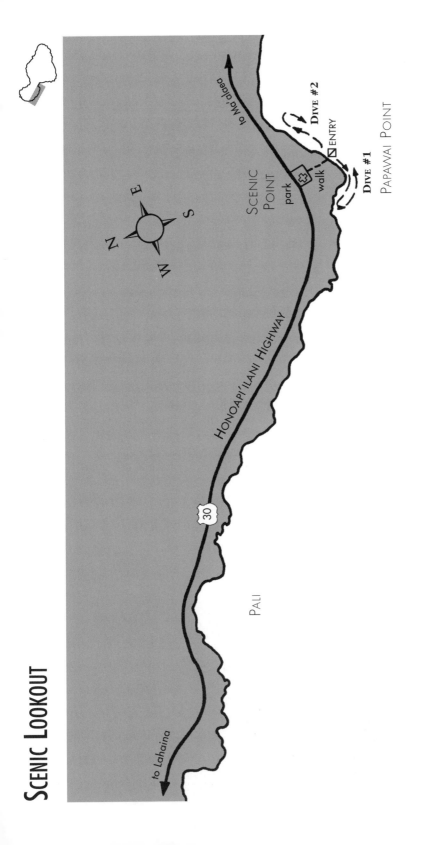

MANU'OHULE (Wash Rock)

ACTIVITY SCUBA

SKILL LEVEL Beginner to Intermediate Level Divers

DEPTH 25 feet around the wash rock, but as deep as 45 feet off to the left (east) of the wash rock.

TRANSPORTATION A car is fine if you park by the road.

DIRECTIONS Travel .5 mile to the east (toward Kahului) from the Scenic Lookout. Look for the jeep trail down to the right (ocean side, naturally). Park at the top if you have anything less than a jeep and walk down (8.1 mile marker).

WHEN YEAR-ROUND, when calm.

WHERE TO DIVE Go straight out around the wash rock. Then head to the right to look for an underwater arch or go left and cruise some underwater mountain ranges varying from 20 to 50 feet in depth.

WHAT TO EXPECT Intricate detail and good relief around the wash rock. The large "mountain ranges" off to the left are covered with coral. The area supports a good population of reef fish. Look for the underwater arch about twenty yards out and to the right, on a 45 degree angle from the wash rock.

HAZARDS The entry can be dangerous if there's surf coming in.

FACILITIES Nothing.

COMMENTS Pick your own entry. I prefer over to the west (right as you face the water). No wet suit is necessary if the water is calm.

Pick your own entry here.

MANU'OHULE & McGREGOR POINT

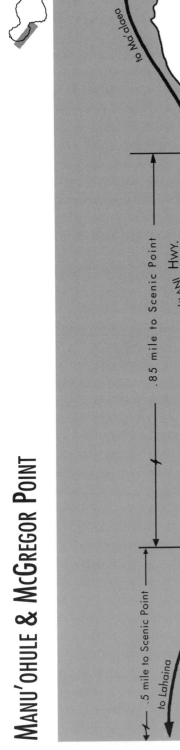

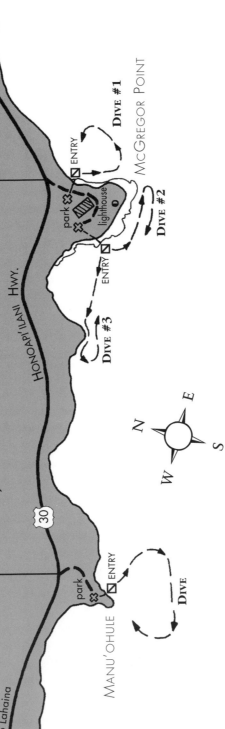

to Ma'alaea

McGREGOR POINT

DIVE #1

ENTRY

park

lighthouse

DIVE #2

ENTRY

.85 mile to Scenic Point

HONOAPI'ILANI HWY.

DIVE #3

N
E
S
W

30

DIVE

park

ENTRY

MANU'OHULE

.5 mile to Scenic Point

to Lahaina

McGregor Point (Lighthouse)

Activity SCUBA

Skill Level Intermediate

Depth DIVE #1.....30 feet
DIVE #2.....40 to 50 feet
DIVE #3.....35 feet

Transportation Car

Directions From the Scenic Lookout, go east for .85 miles. Turn off to the right (ocean side) on a gravel road leading to the lighthouse. Park as soon as you turn in for DIVE #1. Drive in a little further for DIVES #2 and #3 (7.6 mile marker).

When YEAR-ROUND.

Where to Dive Check the map. I like to dive #2 the best.

What to Expect Colorful reef at all three sites even though they're not too extensive. The usual population of reef fish inhabit the area and a spiny lobster or two may be found at DIVES #2 and #3 at night. The walk down the hill to the water is fairly steep and tricky at all three sites but the entries aren't bad.

Hazards Mainly the walk down.

Facilities The usual, zero.

Comments Enter off the lava rock shelf for DIVES #2 and #3. Wearing a wet suit or knee pads can really be helpful on the exit.

Entry for DIVES #2 and #3.

KAMAOLE PARK #2 AND KAMAOLE PARK #3

ACTIVITY   Snorkel

SKILL LEVEL   Beginners

DEPTH   25 feet

TRANSPORTATION   Car

DIRECTIONS   It's right across from Kai-Nani Village in Kihei. Approximately a mile and a half south of Foodland.

WHEN   YEAR-ROUND.

WHERE TO DIVE   To the far left of Kamaole Park #2 or the far right of Kamaole Park #3. Just head out in front of the rocks. Whether you approach it from the left or right, it's the same reef.

WHAT TO EXPECT   Coral covers much of the lava rock outcropping under water. Several small but colorful reef fish may be seen.

HAZARDS   None under normal conditions. There's a lifeguard in case of emergency.

FACILITIES   Showers, toilets and picnic tables at Park #2. Add charcoal grills to the list at Park #3.

COMMENTS   As usual, snorkeling is best in the morning.

The dive as seen from Kamaole #3.

ULUA BEACH - MOKAPU BEACH

ACTIVITY SCUBA or Snorkel

SKILL LEVEL Beginner SCUBA divers; Beginner to Intermediate Level Snorkelers

DEPTH 35 feet maximum at the outer reef

TRANSPORTATION Car

DIRECTIONS Going toward Makena from Kihei, it's the next right after the Stouffer Wailea Beach Resort. If you pass the Intercontinental Hotel, you've gone too far.

WHEN YEAR-ROUND.

WHERE TO DIVE Circle the rock outcrop jutting out between Ulua and Mokapu Beach, or go straight out to the outer reef directly in front of these rocks.

WHAT TO EXPECT You'll find two reef areas; the obvious inner one and another further out. Both support plenty of marine life and an occasional slipper lobster may be found on the outer reef at night. The outer reef is a little too deep for Snorkelers. You'll most likely need a tank.

HAZARDS None I can think of.

FACILITIES Shower and toilets.

COMMENTS The entry is easy. You might consider night diving here too.

Rocky area separating Ulua Beach and Mokapu Beach.

ULUA BEACH - MOKAPU BEACH

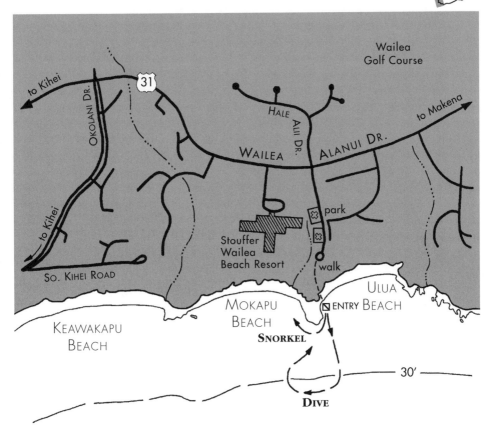

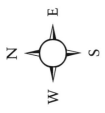

WAILEA BEACH/POLO BEACH

ACTIVITY

POLO: Snorkel
WAILEA: Snorkel or SCUBA

SKILL LEVEL

Beginner to Intermediate Divers and Snorkelers at both sites

DEPTH

POLO: 20 to 30 feet
WAILEA: The reef runs out at 50 feet

TRANSPORTATION

Car

DIRECTIONS

WAILEA: Going toward Makena from Kihei, pass the Intercontinental Hotel and the Wailea Shopping Village. 3/10 mile
past the Shopping Village, look for the sign on your right side
for Wailea Beach and turn right down an access road leading to
a paved parking lot. It's just before the Four Seasons Resort.
Walk down to the beach and go all the way over to your left
(south) to the lava rock out-cropping.
POLO: Going from Kihei toward Makena, turn right 4/10 of a
mile after the Wailea Beach turn-off on to Kaukahi Street, just
past the Kea Lani Hotel. Go to the bottom of the hill and turn
right again into the Polo Beach parking lot.

WHEN

YEAR-ROUND.

WHERE TO DIVE

Snorkeling to the right of Polo Beach or to the left of Wailea Beach
will get you to the safe reef area. Divers should head straight out
from the point to deeper water and a fairly large reef area
fizzling out at the 50 ft. depth. There's also a reef system to the
south of Polo Beach, but it's not as colorful nor is the relief as good.

WHAT TO EXPECT

Plenty of fish in close to the rocks and even more fish further
out. MU, UKU, ARGUS GROUPER, PALANI, A'AWA, PO'OU and
other edible species may be encountered along with several
other inedible varieties.

HAZARDS

None, as long as the surf is low.

FACILITIES

Showers and toilets at both beach parks.

COMMENTS

Both beaches can be super for sun-bathing. Divers from Wailea
Beach should enter from the sand beach and snorkel out to the
point before descending to conserve air for the dive.

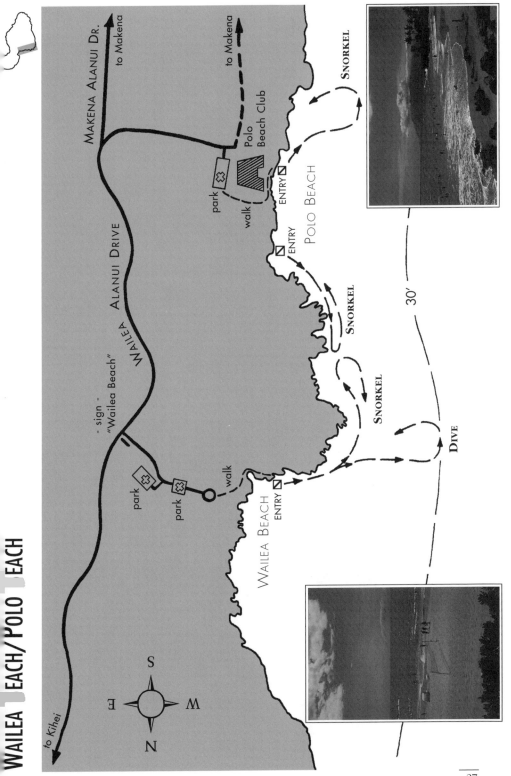

HALOA POINT

ACTIVITY	SCUBA
SKILL LEVEL	Beginner to Intermediate Level Divers
DEPTH	50 feet maximum
TRANSPORTATION	Car
DIRECTIONS	Coming from Kihei: Head south past Wailea on Wailea Alanui Drive. Turn right on Kaukahi St. heading toward the Polo Beach Club. At the bottom of the hill turn left on Makena Road and go for 1/3 mile to Palauea Beach. Park alongside the road and walk to the left (south) end of the beach.
WHEN	YEAR-ROUND.
WHERE TO DIVE	Follow the trail at the south end of the beach a short ways further and enter from the coral rubble beach. Head straight out for approximately 50 yards and then angle off on a 45 degree angle to the left. Cross over a brief patch of sand bottom to reach the outer reef.
WHAT TO EXPECT	The reef area is fairly large with plenty of marine life. TURTLES, EELS, RAYS, several TROPICAL FISH, and even a few species of edible fish can be found here. The relief is quite good at the outer reef with plenty of irregularity.
HAZARDS	The entry can be dangerous if the surf is crashing in.
FACILITIES	Not a thing.
COMMENTS	Access to this beach has been restricted off and on over the years. It may not be open when you show up.

Dive out in front of these lava fingers.

HALOA POINT

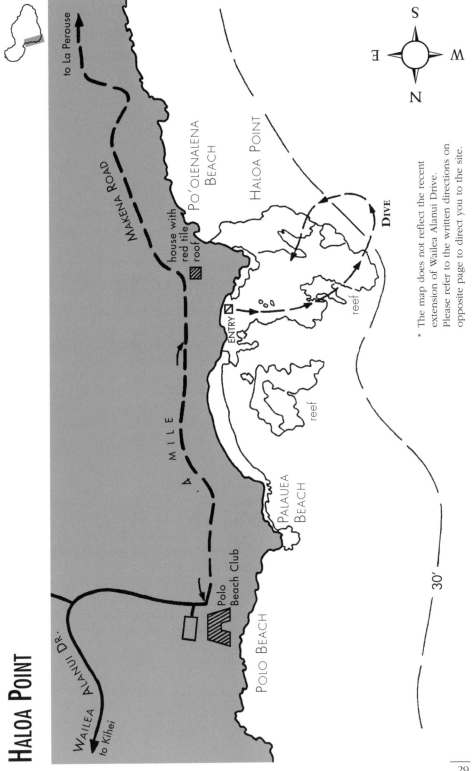

* The map does not reflect the recent extension of Wailea Alanui Drive. Please refer to the written directions on opposite page to direct you to the site.

29

NAHUNA POINT (The Five Graves)

ACTIVITY SCUBA mainly, but you can snorkel here too if you like. You'll need tanks to get down to the caves, though.

SKILL LEVEL Intermediate Level Divers and Advanced Level Cave Divers

DEPTH 40 to 50 feet maximum

TRANSPORTATION Car

DIRECTIONS Heading south from Kihei on Makena Alanui Dr., keep your eyes open for the Makena Surf Condominiums. Just past this landmark, turn right on Makena Road and proceed 2/10 mile to a short dirt road on the right leading to a small graveyard. Park here and suit up.

WHEN YEAR-ROUND; first thing in the morning.

WHERE TO DIVE Follow the short rock-lined foot path to the water where you'll see a small protected cove for your entry. Head straight out from here. Follow along the right side of the wall, looking for the caves as you go. Check the map for further details.

WHAT TO EXPECT Look for several underwater caves and a resident WHITE-TIPPED REEF SHARK. Some of the caves go back for incredible distances but have little life in them. The reef area is fairly irregular and colorful and supports a few SPINY LOBSTERS and a few varieties of reef fish. TURTLES are also fairly common here.

HAZARDS The resident shark isn't a problem, but he may scare you to death if you bump into him as you make your way through the caves. Much more dangerous than that is the possibility of getting yourself wedged in one of the caves. We all know how tempting it is to crawl in as far as is humanly possible, but it's not too much fun getting stuck.

FACILITIES A graveyard, in case you don't make it. 2/10 mile further at Makena Landing are showers and restrooms.

COMMENTS One of the best dives in the area.

NAHUNA POINT (The Five Graves)

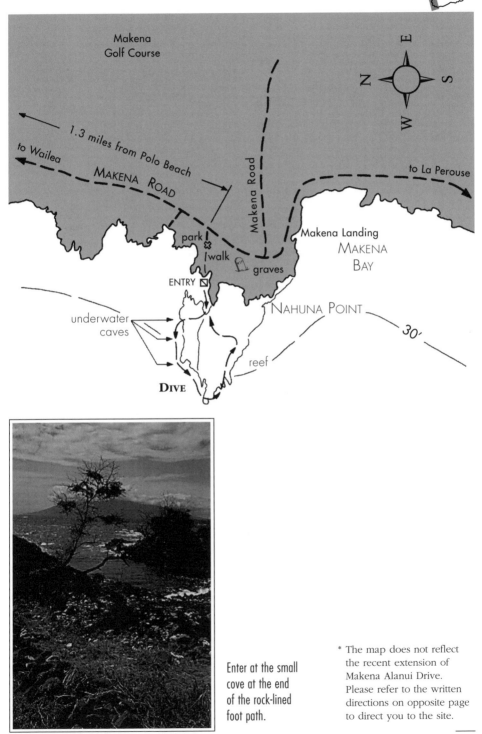

Makena
Golf Course

N E S W (compass)

1.3 miles from Polo Beach

to Wailea

MAKENA ROAD

Makena Road

to La Perouse

Makena Landing

MAKENA BAY

park

walk

graves

ENTRY

underwater caves

NAHUNA POINT

30'

reef

DIVE

Enter at the small
cove at the end
of the rock-lined
foot path.

* The map does not reflect
the recent extension of
Makena Alanui Drive.
Please refer to the written
directions on opposite page
to direct you to the site.

MOLOKINI ISLAND

ACTIVITY   SCUBA or Snorkel

SKILL LEVEL   Beginner Snorkelers to Advanced Divers

DEPTH   100 ft. maximum inside the crater and reported as deep as 400 ft. to sand bottom on the back wall.

TRANSPORTATION   Boat from Maui.

DIRECTIONS   Leave that to the boat captain.

WHEN   YEAR-ROUND.

WHERE TO DIVE   DIVE #1: Range from 30 to 100 ft. on the inside of the crater. Follow your instincts and the concentration of fish.
DIVE #2: Drop down to as deep as 160 ft. to check out the white-tipped reef sharks on the point of Molokini nearest Maui.
DIVE #3: Range from one side of the island to the other side with your boat following from above to pick you up when you ascend.
DIVE #4: Anchor your boat inside the submerged extension of Molokini's northwest tip. Enter here and head over the shoal to over 100 ft. of water.

WHAT TO EXPECT   Molokini Island is a marine-life conservation district and you can expect to see myriad's of varieties of reef fish in moderate abundance. Although too numerous to list all of the species present, let me mention a few. WHITE-TIPPED REEF SHARKS are the main attraction. Large MANTA RAYS and EAGLE RAYS are also common. TURTLES, EELS, SPINNER DOLPHINS, NENUE, LEMON BUTTER-FISH, GOAT FISH, VARIOUS JACKS (ULUA), TRUMPET FISH, UHU, VARIOUS SURGEON FISH and a host of others are sure to be encountered with varying degrees of regularity. DIVE #3 isn't very colorful but is awesome to experience the sheer drop of Molokini's back wall.

HAZARDS   Beware of strong currents on any of the dives other than inside the crater. Watch your depth carefully when cruising the back side. It's easy to find yourself dropping to depths much deeper than you want to be. DIVE #2 is a DECOMPRESSION DIVE. Consult your Navy Tables and allow plenty of air for decompression stops.

COMMENTS   I realize Molokini is not a shore dive, but in case you get the chance to take a boat out there, this should give you an idea of some of the diving available. Remember, Molokini is another GAME PRESERVE. No spearing or collecting. Also, PLEASE refrain from feeding the fish and express your disgust to divemasters who intend to feed the eels. This childish and archaic activity confuses their behavioral patterns making them much more vulnerable to predators and hastens their demise.

MOLOKINI ISLAND

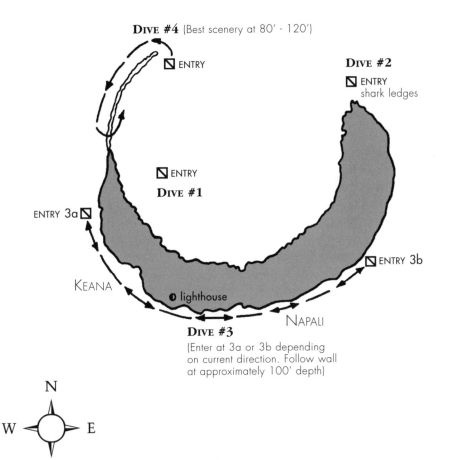

DIVE #4 (Best scenery at 80' - 120')

☒ ENTRY

DIVE #2
☒ ENTRY
shark ledges

☒ ENTRY
DIVE #1

ENTRY 3a ☒

☒ ENTRY 3b

KEANA

❶ lighthouse

NAPALI

DIVE #3
(Enter at 3a or 3b depending
on current direction. Follow wall
at approximately 100' depth)

N
W ← → E
S

ONEULI BEACH/MAKENA BEACH

ACTIVITY
ONEULI: SCUBA
MAKENA: Snorkel

SKILL LEVEL
Intermediate Level Divers and Snorkelers

DEPTH
ONEULI: 20 to 30 feet
MAKENA: 30 to 40 feet

TRANSPORTATION
Car with good ground clearance

DIRECTIONS
ONEULI: Heading south on Makena Alanui Dr. watch for the Maui Prince Hotel. Continue .85 miles past the hotel entrance to a dirt road with an iron entry gate on the right leading to the ocean. MAKENA: 1 mile past the Prince Hotel entrance and .15 miles past the entrance to Oneuli Beach, turn right on a paved road leading to a parking area for Makena Beach. Walk down the beach to the right and over the hill on the north end of "Big Beach." Here you'll find another "Little Beach." Cross this clothing optional beach and enter on its far north end.

WHEN
YEAR-ROUND.

WHERE TO DIVE
ONEULI: Head to the south and follow the coral formations under water. MAKENA: Continue to the north once you make your entry. Snorkelers can also enter the water from Big Beach and snorkel around to "Little Beach."

WHAT TO EXPECT
Here's another of the best snorkeling areas on this side of the island. The relief is interesting with several fingers and valleys protruding out perpendicularly to the coastline. You're likely to encounter schools of MU, MOANA, UHU, PALANI, A'AWA, and various other inedible species. You're also likely to scare up a SLIPPER or SPINY LOBSTER now and then. Most of the area can be explored with snorkel gear though some of the reef gets too deep for most people's breath-hold ability. It's a long way to pack your tank from the Makena side. I'd recommend you check it out with snorkel gear first.

HAZARDS
ONEULI: Rough surf can make the entry dangerous.
MAKENA: Beware of the possiblity of currents.

FACILITIES
Occasionally a garbage can and now a toilet.

COMMENTS
A wet suit is not necessary at "Little Beach." In fact, you won't even need a swimsuit.

ONEULI BEACH/MAKENA BEACH

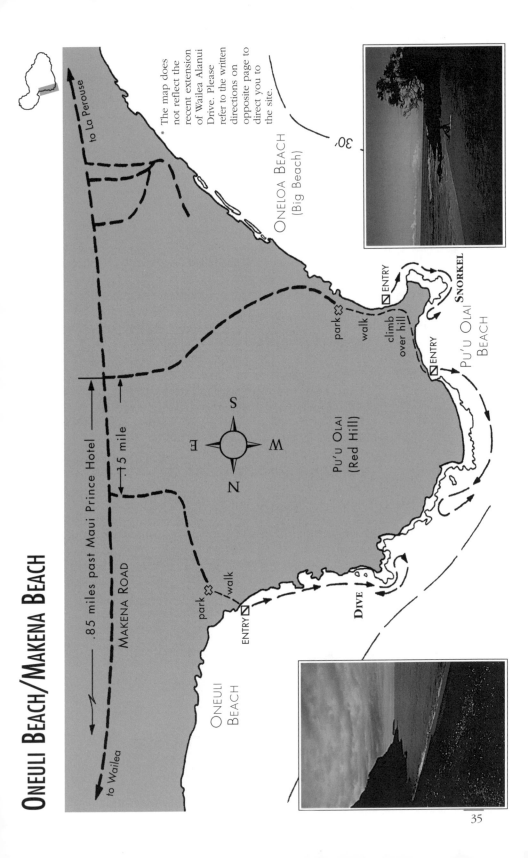

* The map does not reflect the recent extension of Wailea Alanui Drive. Please refer to the written directions on opposite page to direct you to the site.

ONELOA BEACH
(Big Beach)

30'

to La Perouse

.85 miles past Maui Prince Hotel

MAKENA ROAD

.15 mile

to Wailea

S

E ✦ W

N

PU'U OLAI
(Red Hill)

park ✕ walk

ENTRY ☑

ONEULI
BEACH

DIVE

park ✕ walk

climb over hill

☑ ENTRY

☑ ENTRY

PU'U OLAI SNORKEL
BEACH

Ahihi Cove

ACTIVITY	Snorkel
SKILL LEVEL	Beginner to Intermediate
DEPTH	5 to 30 feet
TRANSPORTATION	Car
DIRECTIONS	Travel south past the Maui Prince Hotel for approximately 2 miles until you see the sign for the "Ahihi Kinau Reserve." Continue 1/10 mile further and pull off alongside the road right at the small cove.
WHEN	YEAR-ROUND except during periods of large swells.
WHERE TO DIVE	Head straight out bearing a bit to the left and follow the highest concentration of coral reef.
WHAT TO EXPECT	An amazing variety of reef fishes including: ARGUS GROUPER, WEKE, BLUE LINED SNAPPER, TRUMPET FISH, RUDDER FISH, PALANI, AKULE, DAMSEL FISH, MANINI, BUTTERFLY FISH, WRASSE, UHU (PARROT FISH), several species of SURGEON FISHES and others.
HAZARDS	Possibly urchins in shallow water.
FACILITIES	None.
COMMENTS	Remember, this is part of a natural area preserve. You can look but not touch.

Enter here.

AHIHI COVE

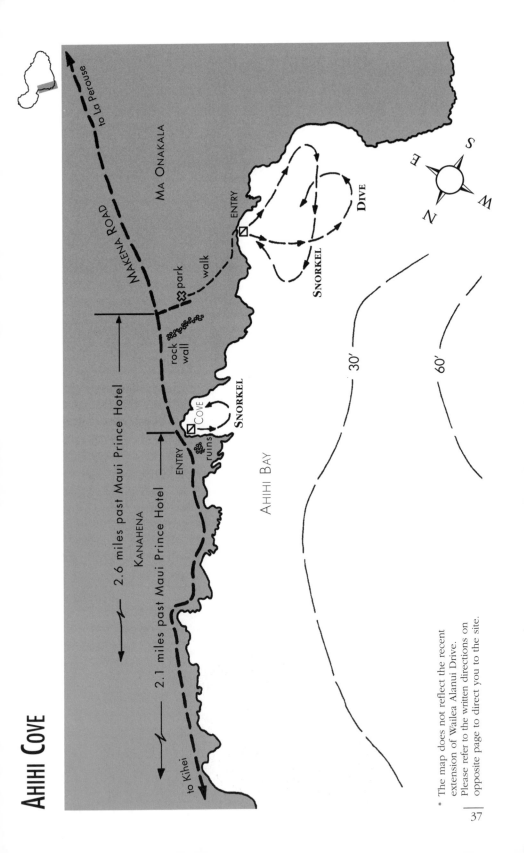

to La Perouse

MAKENA ROAD

MA ONAKALA

ENTRY

park

walk

ENTRY

SNORKEL

DIVE

rock
wall

ruins

COVE

SNORKEL

AHIHI BAY

30'

60'

— 2.6 miles past Maui Prince Hotel —

KANAHENA

— 2.1 miles past Maui Prince Hotel —

to Kihei

S

E

W

N

* The map does not reflect the recent
extension of Wailea Alanui Drive.
Please refer to the written directions on
opposite page to direct you to the site.

AHIHI BAY

ACTIVITY	SCUBA or Snorkel
SKILL LEVEL	Beginner to Intermediate Level Divers and Snorkelers
DEPTH	20 feet over most of the reef area. Reef hits sand bottom at approximately 55 feet.
TRANSPORTATION	Car
DIRECTIONS	Travel 2.6 miles past the Maui Prince Hotel heading south, where you'll reach a gravel road on your right leading to the water. Drive in about 75 feet and park. The best entry spot is just a short distance to your left (south).
WHEN	YEAR-ROUND; may be better in the WINTER.
WHERE TO DIVE	Head straight out from your entry point and circle around toward the left hand side of the bay. Divers can head out to deeper water. Snorkelers can range within their free diving ability.
WHAT TO EXPECT	You'll find an extremely colorful reef, replete with several distinct varieties of coral. Several varieties of REEF FISH, STAR FISH, URCHINS, EELS and SHELLS are present. This is a part of a natural area reserve, though, so please refrain from taking anything.
HAZARDS	Nothing, if the water is calm.
FACILITIES	None.
COMMENTS	This is another excellent spot for a night dive. There's no wall to follow on this one though. You'll need a compass and a light burning on shore to guide yourself back out. If there's a full moon, you'll hardly need a light. The intricate detail of the various corals can really be appreciated at night.

Pick your own entry.

AHIHI BAY

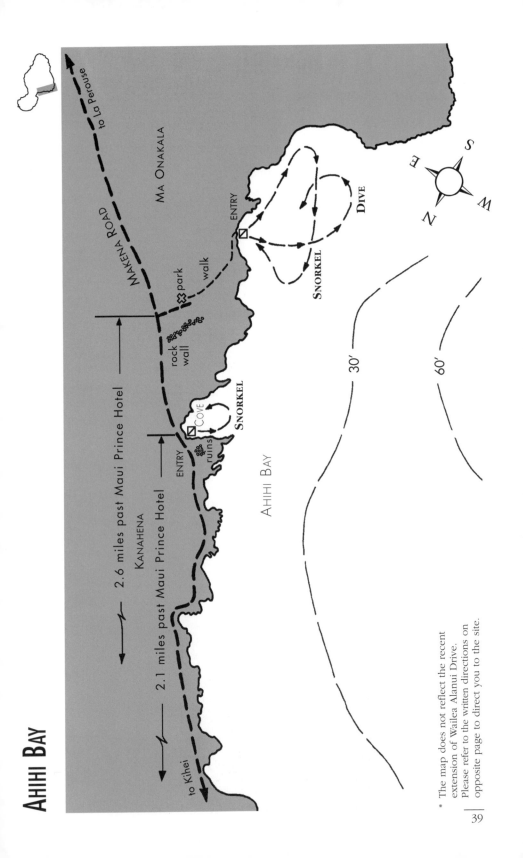

* The map does not reflect the recent
  extension of Wailea Alanui Drive.
  Please refer to the written directions on
  opposite page to direct you to the site.

La Perouse Bay

ACTIVITY SCUBA or Snorkel

SKILL LEVEL Beginner to Intermediate Level Divers and Snorkelers

DEPTH 15 to 30 feet along the wall to the north; 30 to 50 feet out in the bay

TRANSPORTATION Car with good ground clearance

DIRECTIONS Continue south for 4 miles past the Maui Prince Hotel. Here you'll find a short gravel road leading to the right. Follow it as close to the ocean as possible and park.

WHEN The entry can be fairly well protected YEAR-ROUND.

WHERE TO DIVE Enter where the scraggly barbed-wire fence meets the water. Head over to your right and work in and out of the lava fingers of Cape Kina'u. Alternately, you can head to deeper water in the middle of the bay.

WHAT TO EXPECT Here you'll find a moderate sampling of reef fish. A few EELS, including a TIGER MORAY, PARROT FISH, PORCUPINE FISH, and plenty of LIZARD FISH may be found with a little scrutiny. The relief near the wall is decent with intricately detailed coral. The bottom out in the middle of the bay is fairly flat with coral interspersed with sand bottom. The further out you go the sand is replaced by more coral and with better relief. A typical population of reef fish inhabit the area such as TRUMPETS AND SURGEON FISH.

HAZARDS Urchins in the shallow water entry can be painful when stepped on. I'd recommend hard-soled booties. Don't dive if the surf is up.

FACILITIES Not a thing.

COMMENTS This is as far as you can go with a car. Visibility is usually better at Ahihi Bay.

Enter here.

LA PEROUSE BAY

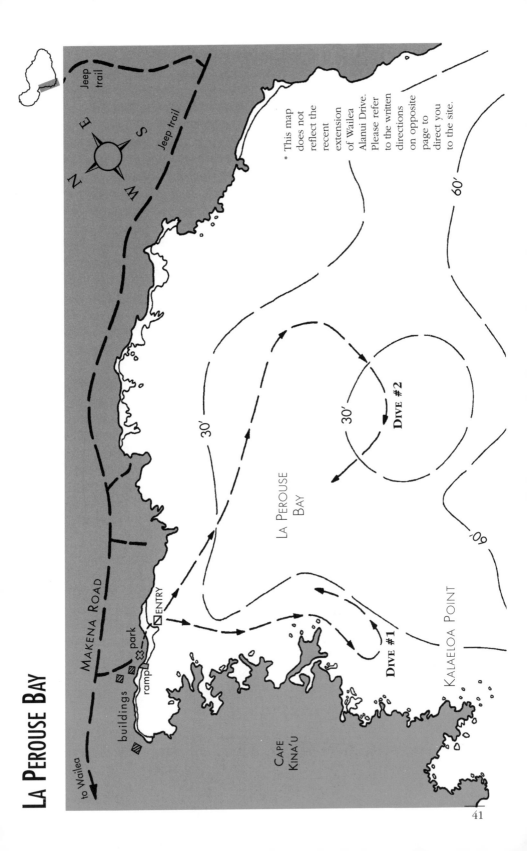

to Wailea

MAKENA ROAD

Jeep trail

Jeep trail

buildings

park

ramp

ENTRY

CAPE KINA'U

LA PEROUSE BAY

DIVE #1

KALAELOA POINT

DIVE #2

30'

30'

60'

60'

* This map does not reflect the recent extension of Wailea Alanui Drive. Please refer to the written directions on opposite page to direct you to the site.

KAHAWAIHAPAPA POINT

ACTIVITY   SCUBA

SKILL LEVEL   Advanced Divers, skilled in rough water entries; also certified Cave Divers

DEPTH   Approximately 50 feet to the edge of the reef

TRANSPORTATION   Jeep or 4x4 Truck

DIRECTIONS   Turn down the dirt road off the Pi'ilani Highway at the 26.5 mile marker. Drive all the way down bearing to the left. Walk straight down onto the lava rock finger protruding out into the ocean. Enter on the left side of this finger.

WHEN   Almost exclusively during the WINTER.

WHERE TO DIVE   Once you're in the water, head down the coast to your right (west) to get to the best relief. You'll need to swim a couple hundred feet across the bay to get to the three underwater caves (DIVE #2). Head to the east to locate some small caves and more good spear fishing grounds. The caves are all located in the 25 to 30 ft. depth range, but some are quite lengthy and can be quite dangerous due to surge and deteriorating visibility for the return trip (they're one way caves). If you're not a certified cave diver, keep out!

WHAT TO EXPECT   You'll find the caves stuffed with MENPACHI and SQUIRREL FISH. SPINY LOBSTERS are no stranger to the caves either. The largest of the two caves ends up at a small air chamber when the tide is low. It's large enough for 2 or 3 divers to crawl up in, remove their masks and regulators, and relax awhile.

HAZARDS   The entry is difficult even for experienced divers. Large seas can make the entry extremely dangerous and the dive should not be attempted under these conditions. Incidentally, the walk down is also not for the squeamish.

FACILITIES   You'd better bring your own toilet paper here.

COMMENTS   The water must be ideal to get in here. It's an excellent dive and well worth the effort, but it's nice to go home in one piece. I wouldn't dive here without a full wet suit for protection.

KAHAWAIHAPAPA POINT

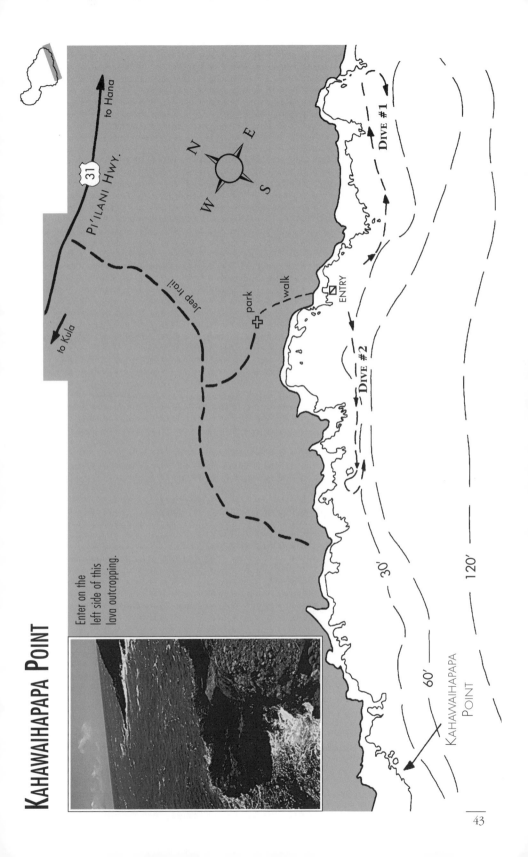

Enter on the left side of this lava outcropping.

P'ILANI HWY.

to Hana

31

to Kula

Jeep trail

park

walk

ENTRY

DIVE #1

DIVE #2

30'

60'

120'

KAHAWAIHAPAPA POINT

NU'U BAY

ACTIVITY   SCUBA or Snorkel

SKILL LEVEL   Intermediate to Advanced Divers and Snorkelers

DEPTH   110 feet out to sand bottom where the reef runs out

TRANSPORTATION   Truck or car

DIRECTIONS   Taking the south route toward Hana on Hwy. #31, look for a green gate at the 30.9 mile marker. It's one of the few that aren't locked. Lift up the wire loop, open the gate, go through, and re-hook the wire loop. Then drive in the rest of the way.

WHEN   YEAR-ROUND but best in WINTER.

WHERE TO DIVE   Walk a short ways to Nono'u Bay for your entry and snorkel out a bit to save air. Drop down just before you round the corner to the left, continue east (to the left), and angle off to deeper water. Look for the large rock outcroppings along the way where most of the fish congregate.

WHAT TO EXPECT   One of the best dives on the south side of the island. Definitely your *ace in the hole* for this side. Nu'u Bay is well protected from summer's trade winds and winter's northwest swell. The reef here is very extensive and drops off quickly to depths of over 100 feet. Look for giant ULUA often over 100 pounds, AWAS commonly 4 to 6 ft. long, KAHALA, PAPIO, GROUPER, UHU, PO'OU, A'AWA, PALANI, PUALU, UKU, SPINY LOBSTER and HAMMERHEAD, TIGER and GREY REEF SHARKS. LARGE MANTA RAYS, EAGLE RAYS, SPINNER DOLPHINS, MORAY EELS, and TURTLES can also be spotted on occasion. Visibility ranges from 15 to 80 ft. and averages about 40 ft.

HAZARDS   Current running due to tide changes is usually heading to the east. This can make your return trip to the exit a problem. If the current is running, be sure to allow more than half your air to get back in.

FACILITIES   The remains of an old cattle launch.

COMMENTS   Only during periods of south swell does Nu'u become too rough to dive. Stand on the high rocks and check the water clarity before entering. This dive has one of the easiest entry/exit spots on this side of the island and one of the shortest walks from the parking area to the entry. It's a good dive if you're out of shape or haven't kicked the smoking habit.

NU'U BAY

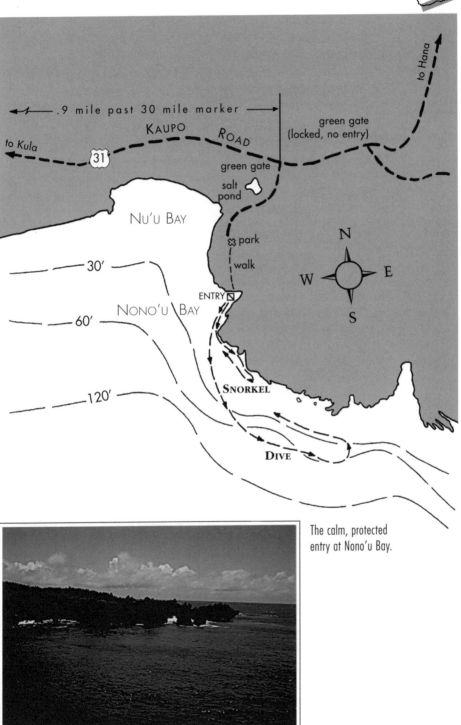

to Hana

.9 mile past 30 mile marker

KAUPO ROAD

to Kula

31

green gate
(locked, no entry)

green gate

salt
pond

NU'U BAY

park

walk

N

W   E

S

30'

NONO'U BAY

ENTRY

60'

120'

SNORKEL

DIVE

The calm, protected
entry at Nono'u Bay.

HALEKI'I

ACTIVITY   SCUBA

SKILL LEVEL   Intermediate to Advanced Divers at either spot

DEPTH   DIVE #1: 30 ft. to 80 ft.
DIVE #2: 30 ft. to 35 ft.

TRANSPORTATION   Car with good ground clearance

DIRECTIONS   Heading east toward Hana on the Pi'ilani Hwy., turn right at the 35.5 mile marker. Follow this dirt and gravel road down to the Hui Aloha Church and the water. Head back up to the main road and continue for another .45 miles to the turnoff for DIVE #2. Coming from Hana, go approximately 7/10 mile past the 36 mile marker and turn left onto the gravel road leading to the church.

WHEN   Best in the WINTER, but even then only on a good day.

WHERE TO DIVE   Out in front of the rocks for DIVE #1; drive or swim over to your left for DIVE #2 (see map).

WHAT TO EXPECT   One of the best dives in the book with a fairly safe entry (depending on conditions). The small wash rock islands off-shore continue further out forming interesting and irregular relief in the 30 ft. to 80 ft. depth range. Several varieties of fish inhabit the area, including UKU, PAPIO, NENUE, OMILU, MOANO, UHU, ULUA, MU, NOHU and dozens of reef fish. The spiny lobster population is rather sparse, due no doubt to the accessibility of the spot. DIVE #2 has less relief but is still a colorful reef area to explore when the ocean swells permit entry.

HAZARDS   Rough seas make the area inaccessible during most of the year, especially summer. There are times during the winter, though, when the seas really flatten out. I wouldn't dive here unless it's one of those days.

FACILITIES   Nothing. So, what else is new?

COMMENTS   I would definitely bring a wet suit for DIVE #2. DIVE #1 affords a much safer entry and may not require one.

HALEKI'I

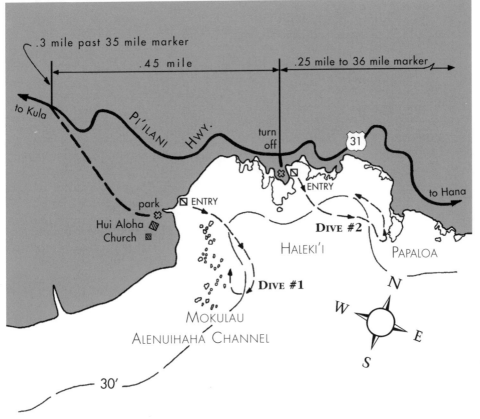

.3 mile past 35 mile marker

.45 mile

.25 mile to 36 mile marker

to Kula

PI'ILANI HWY.

turn off

31

to Hana

ENTRY

park

ENTRY

Hui Aloha Church

DIVE #2

HALEKI'I

PAPALOA

DIVE #1

N

MOKULAU

W

E

ALENUIHAHA CHANNEL

S

30'

Overlooking the Bay at Haleki'i.

OHEO GULCH (Seven Sacred Pools)

ACTIVITY SCUBA

SKILL LEVEL Advanced Divers

DEPTH Generally about 30 to 40 feet; 60 is about the deepest you'll need to go

TRANSPORTATION Car

DIRECTIONS Past Hana, continue to the south for about forty-five minutes. Coming from the west, it's approximately the 41.3 mile marker. You'll know your're there when you get to all the activity, and see the sign *Haleakala National Park*. Drive down to the camping area and park as near as you can to your entry.

WHEN It's usually quite rough here since this side of the island faces directly into the seas built up by the strong easterly winds so common here on Maui. When the marine forecast is calling for 2 to 4 foot seas in coastal areas you've got a chance. The odds of this happening are better in the FALL or WINTER.

WHERE TO DIVE Out in front of the points near Ka'u Bay or over toward Kuloa Point. Check the map.

WHAT TO EXPECT Some really interesting underwater formations; large arches, caves, etc. Not particularly colorful coral but a good population of reef fish can be found. Large ULUA, PAPIO, NENUE, A'AWA, UHU, MOANA, and many others are likely to be spotted. There are some semi-safe entry/exit spots on the leeward side of the lava fingers jutting out into the ocean. You should definitely be wearing a full wet suit for protection. Bring a light to check the holes for lobster.

HAZARDS Only the huge crashing surf pounding in on the shoreline making the entries death-defying.

FACILITIES Toilets, camping, and a hiking trail up to several more waterfalls. Jump in the pools themselves to rinse off the salt water.

COMMENTS Be sure of the safety of your entry spot before committing yourself. If it looks too rough, it probably is. It's seldom safe here, but it's worth diving when it is. If you can't get in there's plenty of other things you can do; go swim in the pools, jump off the rocks into the pools, or hike the trail through the bamboo forest to the 200 foot waterfall, Waimoku Falls, at the end of the trail. If you do plan on diving, the park rangers require that you check in with them first and notify them of your dive plans.

OHEO GULCH (Seven Sacred Pools) - Haleakala National Park

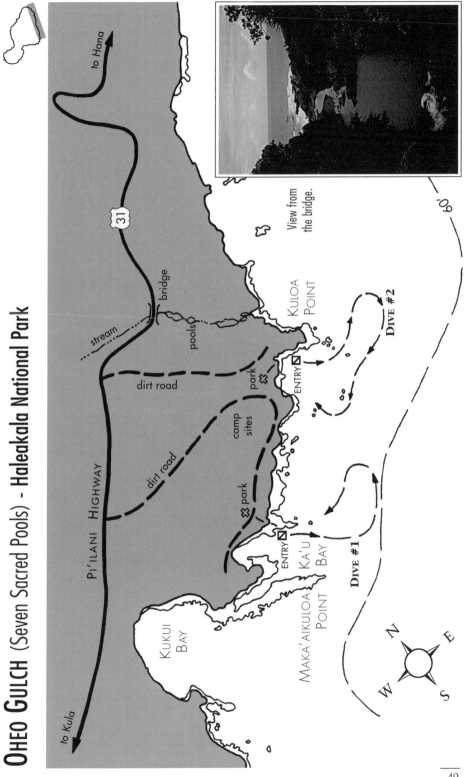

View from the bridge.

to Hana

31

PI'ILANI HIGHWAY

to Kula

bridge

stream

dirt road

dirt road

pools

park

camp sites

park

ENTRY

ENTRY

KULOA POINT

KA'U BAY

MAKA'AIKULOA POINT

KUKUI BAY

DIVE #1

DIVE #2

60'

N
W   E
S

KAIHALULU BEACH (Red Sand Beach)

ACTIVITY   Snorkel

SKILL LEVEL   Beginner to Advanced

DEPTH   5 to 15 feet inside the breakwater

TRANSPORTATION   Car

DIRECTIONS   When you first arrive in Hana the road forks at the police station. Take the left fork (Ua Kea Rd.) and follow it straight through Hana town, past Hana Bay until it dead ends at the Hana Hotel Sea Ranch cottages. DO NOT park here. Double back a bit where you'll find some public parking near the baseball field or tennis courts. Now walk toward the ocean between the Sea Ranch cottages and the Hana Community Center (long green building). You will find a narrow slippery trail skirting the cottages and then along the ocean leading to a gorgeous and secluded red sand beach with a natural lava breakwater protecting an area for safe swimming and snorkeling year-round.

WHEN   YEAR-ROUND; best before 3PM when the sun goes over the hill.

WHERE TO DIVE   Inside the breakwater.

WHAT TO EXPECT   Loads of fish including UHU, TRUMPET FISH, NEEDLEFISH, WEKE, PAPIO, VARIOUS SURGEON FISH including PALANI, PUALU, and UNICORN FISH, SADDLEBACK WRASSE, LEMON BUTTERFLIES, and a potential of many other species.

HAZARDS   The trail alongside the ocean can be very treacherous with loose rubble on the trail making it very slippery.

FACILITIES   Not a thing.

COMMENTS   After snorkeling you can get an all over tan. (Not legally of course but people have been enjoying the nude sunbathing here for as long as anyone can remember.) The access is through private property. Please behave accordingly and don't park where you'll block anyone in or out.

KAIHALULU BEACH (Red Sand Beach)

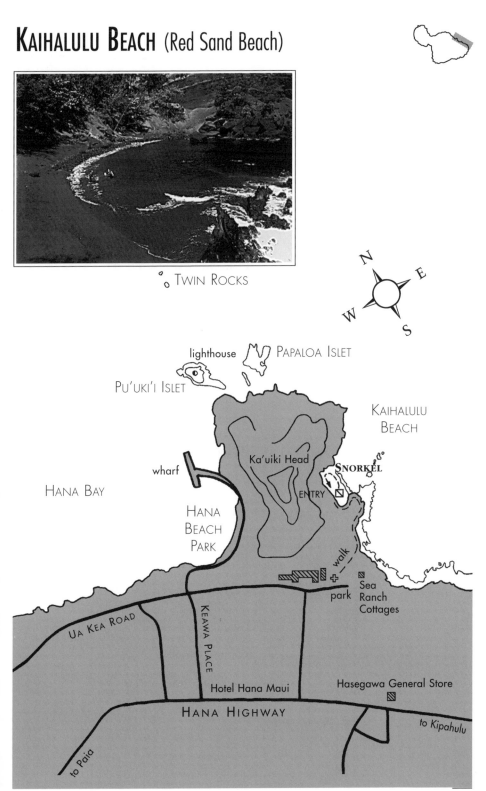

TWIN ROCKS

N
E
W
S

lighthouse   PAPALOA ISLET

PU'UKI'I ISLET

KAIHALULU
BEACH

Ka'uiki Head

wharf   SNORKEL

HANA BAY   ENTRY

HANA
BEACH
PARK

walk

park   Sea
Ranch
Cottages

UA KEA ROAD

KEAWA PLACE

Hotel Hana Maui   Hasegawa General Store

HANA HIGHWAY   to Kipahulu

to Paia

Hana Bay

ACTIVITY	SCUBA or Snorkel
SKILL LEVEL	Beginner Snorkelers, Intermediate to Advanced Divers
DEPTH	15 feet inside for Snorkelers, 60 feet outside
TRANSPORTATION	Car
DIRECTIONS	Take the Hana Hwy. to the furthest point east of the island. Follow the signs into Hana Bay.
WHEN	It's seldom calm here, but your best bet's in WINTER. Snorkelers have a good chance of getting in since Pu'uki'i Island protects this inside area from the ocean. Divers will have to wait for better days to proceed out beyond Pu'uki'i.
WHERE TO DIVE	Snorkelers should stay inside the protection afforded by Pu'uki'i Island. Divers head out around it, straight out and a little to the right.
WHAT TO EXPECT	Really colorful coral inside Pu'uki'i and several species of reef fish. Outside the small island the relief is good but much of the coral is covered with a layer of silt and appears to be dead. Check for a small cave straight out in front of Pu'uki'i Island.
HAZARDS	Rough seas and currents out beyond Pu'uki'i.
FACILITIES	Showers, toilets and a snack counter.
COMMENTS	The entry is easy, but you have to walk a little to get to it. No wet suit is necessary here (except for thermal protection). Snorkelers can look for the anchor not too far from the point of the wharf.

HANA BAY

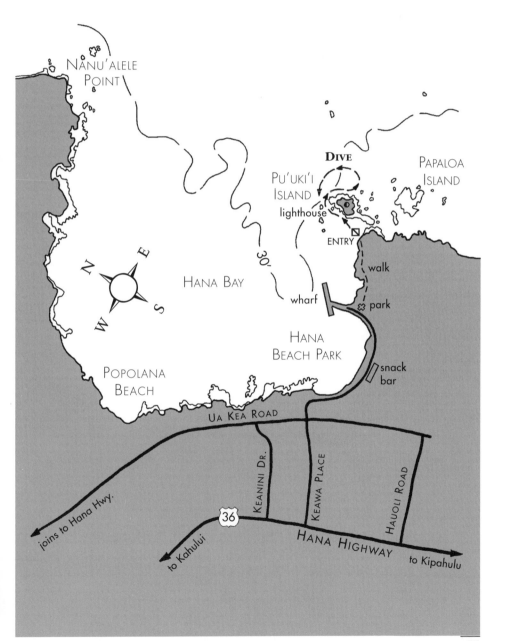

NĀNU'ALELE
POINT

DIVE

PU'UKI'I
ISLAND

PAPALOA
ISLAND

lighthouse

ENTRY

30'

walk

HANA BAY

wharf

park

N

E

S

W

HANA
BEACH PARK

snack
bar

POPOLANA
BEACH

Ua Kea Road

Keanini Dr.

Keawa Place

Hauoli Road

joins to Hana Hwy.

36

to Kahului

HANA HIGHWAY

to Kipahulu

Wai'anapanapa State Park

Activity	SCUBA
Skill Level	Intermediate to Advanced Level Divers
Depth	50 feet is about the maximum
Transportation	Car
Directions	As you're traveling toward Hana on the Hana Hwy., look for the signs for Wai'anapanapa State Park just a couple miles short of Hana itself. Park in the parking area furthest to the left (north). Check the map.
When	You should have more opportunities in the WINTER. Any time there are no marine warnings and the seas are down to 2 ft. in the coastal areas. Check the marine Recorded Forecast for Maui before setting out.
Where to Dive	Enter from the black sand beach and head out to the left along the low sea cliffs. The further you go, the better it gets. If it's really calm, you can snorkel on the right side of the bay out and around the arch and beyond.
What to Expect	The bottom consists of rock and sand bottom out in the middle of the bay and over to the right. You're in for a real surprise, though, if you go out to the left along the low sea cliffs. You'll need to pass the small bay (Keawaiki Bay) on the left before you start getting into the really nice areas. From here on out it just gets better and better. A little irregularity at first soon blossoms into a beautiful and colorful expanse of coral covered mountain ranges with plenty of *pukas* and hiding places for fish and lobster. UKU and MU seems to be plentiful here along with SPINY LOBSTERS and the full gamut of reef fishes. The seas are usually rough here leaving this area seldom diveable. This helps account for the abundance of fish life. Here I've also encountered the somewhat rare and elusive BOAR FISH.
Hazards	Surf funneling into the bay can create strong rip currents pulling back out to sea, EVEN WHEN SEAS ARE SMALL! Unless you're a very strong swimmer, allow plenty of air to return underneath. Never attempt to dive here unless the seas are very small.
Facilities	Picnic tables, showers, toilets, barbecue grills, parking lots, a hiking trail, cabins you can reserve in advance of the night or week (phone 244-4354), and a black sand beach great for sunbathing.
Comments	Check out the wet caves as long as you're here.

WAI'ANAPANAPA STATE PARK

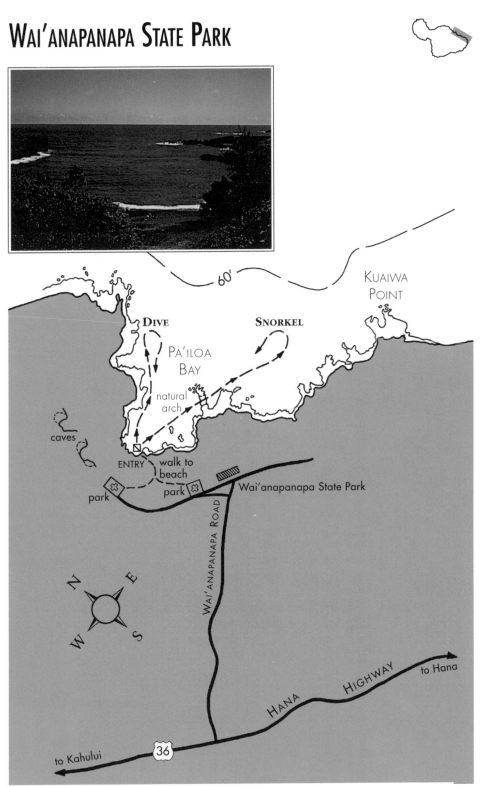

DIVE

SNORKEL

KUAIWA
POINT

PA'ILOA
BAY

60'

natural
arch

caves

ENTRY walk to
beach

park park

Wai'anapanapa State Park

WAI'ANAPANAPA ROAD

N
E
W
S

HANA HIGHWAY

to Hana

36

to Kahului

KAELUA (Nahiku)

ACTIVITY	SCUBA
SKILL LEVEL	Intermediate to Advanced Level Divers
DEPTH	40 to 60 feet
TRANSPORTATION	Car
DIRECTIONS	Going toward Hana on the Hana Hwy., turn left at the 25.1 mile marker. Continue down this winding road for 2.5 miles where you will arrive at the ocean. Park at the very end of this road and enter on the lava flow directly in front.
WHEN	Best in the AUTUMN or periods of light trades in the summer.
WHERE TO DIVE	Head straight out beyond the wash rock and continue for an equal distance further. From here bear to the right and follow your instincts under the water. Enter on the left side of the lava flow.
WHAT TO EXPECT	The reef area is extensive, colorful, and irregularly formed. There are plenty of canyons, valleys, ridges, and holes to harbor marine life. Among the 20 to 30 species native to the area, UKU, AWA, A'AWA, MU, KUMU, PUALU, PAPIO, and GREEN SEA TURTLES seem to be fairly common.
HAZARDS	Mainly large seas making the entry dangerous if not impossible for most of the year.
FACILITIES	The usual, none.
COMMENTS	Here's an excellent dive. It's well worth checking out on your way to Hana.

Entry is on the left side of this lava finger.

KAELUA (Nahiku)

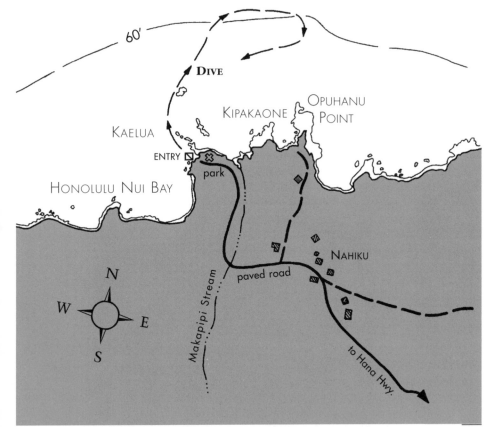

60'

DIVE

KIPAKAONE

OPUHANU POINT

KAELUA

ENTRY

park

HONOLULU NUI BAY

Makapipi Stream

paved road

NAHIKU

N
W   E
S

to Hana Hwy.

KAWE'E POINT (Ke'anae Peninsula)

ACTIVITY	SCUBA
SKILL LEVEL	Intermediate to Advanced Level Divers
DEPTH	30 to 60 feet ranging over the reef
TRANSPORTATION	Car
DIRECTIONS	Going toward Hana on the Hana Hwy., turn left where you see the sign for Ke'anae. This will be at the 16.7 mile marker. From here drive down for .6 miles to Kawe'e Point. Just past the public bathrooms pull off to a gravel parking area on your left.
WHEN	Best in the AUTUMN, when the high trade winds of summer subside and before winter's northwest swell starts up.
WHERE TO DIVE	Enter in the small bay to the south of Kawe'e Point and continue out and around to the left. The reef turns to sand bottom at approximately 60 feet. Follow the formations out to the reef's edge and double back in shallower water.
WHAT TO EXPECT	You'll find another large and colorful reef area with good relief over its entire expanse. Among others, you're likely to see NOHU, ARGUS GROUPER, ULUA, MU, and an occasional SPINY LOBSTER. Spear fishing potential is quite good.
HAZARDS	Summer's trade winds pump large seas directly into this side of Ke'anae Peninsula. This can make the entry impossible and the visibility very poor.
FACILITIES	Restrooms.
COMMENTS	Here's another spot to check out on your way to Hana. If the water is calm, the entry is simple.

The parking and entry at Kawe'e Point.

KAWE'E POINT (Ke'anae Peninsula)

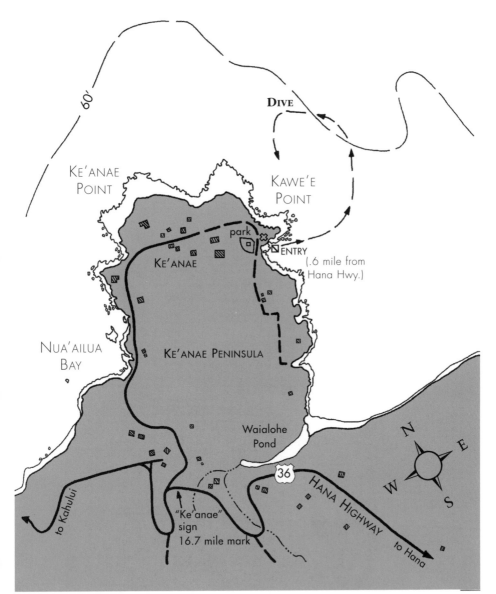

60'

DIVE

KE'ANAE
POINT

KAWE'E
POINT

ENTRY
(.6 mile from
Hana Hwy.)

park

KE'ANAE

Ke'ANAE PENINSULA

NUA'AILUA
BAY

Waialohe
Pond

36

N

E

W

S

to Kahului

HANA HIGHWAY   to Hana

"Ke'anae"
sign
16.7 mile mark

PAUWELA POINT

ACTIVITY SCUBA

SKILL LEVEL DIVE #1: Intermediate
DIVE #2: Advanced
DIVE #3: Advanced

DEPTH Up to 50 feet or more at any of the three areas

TRANSPORTATION Car

DIRECTIONS Going toward Hana, continue 8.4 miles past the intersection with the Haleakala Hwy. (route #37). Look for the sign "Pauwela Lighthouse" just past the Haiku Community Center. Turn left here and head down the long pineapple field road which leads to the lighthouse. If you pass Akahai Street in Pauwela, you've gone too far.

WHEN Best in the SUMMER, sometimes FALL. Also when Kona winds reverse the normal wave patterns in the WINTER.

WHERE TO DIVE There are three different sites you can dive in this area. Check the map.

WHAT TO EXPECT Really colorful reef with good relief at DIVE #2. Mostly rock bottom on DIVE #1 with a few small caves. Lobster hunting at night at DIVE #1 is good. At DIVE #2 look for the rare boar fish, found on the back side of Molokini Crater and a few scattered north shore sites. Spear fishing at any of the three sites is good. At DIVE #3 the bottom starts out as coral and turns into rock bottom in the middle of Wewehi Bay. Decent lobster picking here at night also.

HAZARDS DIVES #2 and #3 are not too well protected from the rough open ocean and the lava rock entries can be difficult and very dangerous when the water is rough. The entry is much better protected at DIVE #1, but the walk down at all three sites is steep and treacherous. In case of a real problem at DIVES #2 and #3, you can always swim all the way to the rock beach at Wewehi Bay. There is a trail back up to your car.

FACILITIES None.

COMMENTS DIVE #1 makes the best night dive. Bring a compass and leave a light burning on shore to mark your exit. It's easy to get turned around. Kama'ainas warn of tiger sharks in the area.

Pauwela Point

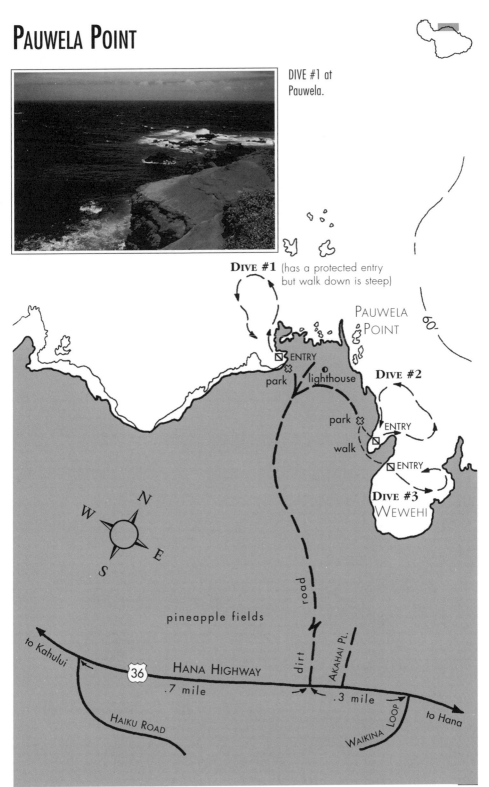

DIVE #1 at Pauwela.

DIVE #1 (has a protected entry but walk down is steep)

PAUWELA POINT

60'

ENTRY

park   lighthouse

DIVE #2

park

ENTRY

walk

ENTRY

DIVE #3
WEWEHI

N
W   E
S

pineapple fields

road

to Kahului

36   HANA HIGHWAY

.7 mile

dirt

AKAHAI PL.

.3 mile

to Hana

HAIKU ROAD

WAIKINA LOOP

MALIKO BAY (Right Side)

ACTIVITY SCUBA

SKILL LEVEL Intermediate Level Divers

DEPTH 70 feet maximum

TRANSPORTATION Car

DIRECTIONS Going toward Hana, continue 6.8 miles past the intersection with the Haleakala Hwy. (route #37). Turn right here and follow the dirt road as it makes a loop back under the highway and straight into Maliko Gulch. Park so as not to interfere with the boat launch and snorkel out to the wash rocks before dropping down; or, follow the miserable excuse for a trail along the right side of the bay and enter off the small boulders, eliminating some surface swimming.

WHEN Best in SUMMER. Check the surf at Hookipa Park on your way. This will help indicate surf conditions at Maliko. If there are no surfing waves, it's likely to be diveable.

WHERE TO DIVE Directly in front of the wash rocks.

WHAT TO EXPECT Out in front of the wash rocks are some very deep crevasses. TURTLES are almost always abundant. UHU, PALANI, A'AWA, NOHU, WEKE, MOANA, VARIOUS SURGEON FISH and others inhabit the area. An occasional SPINY LOBSTER may also be found.

HAZARDS It's a fairly deep dive; be careful to return with plenty of air.

FACILITIES A boat launch.

COMMENTS This site is fairly well protected from the large surf built up by strong predominantly easterly trade winds. A full wet suit for protection may not be necessary.

Launch Ramp at Maliko Bay.

MALIKO BAY (Right Side)

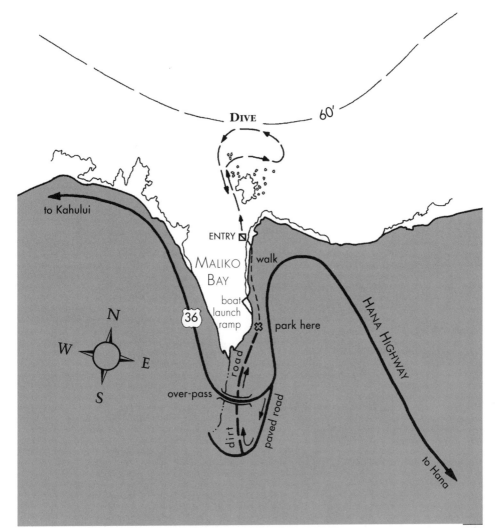

DIVE

60'

to Kahului

ENTRY

MALIKO BAY

walk

boat launch ramp

park here

36

N

W   E

S

over-pass

dirt road

paved road

HANA HIGHWAY

to Hana

MALIKO BAY (Left Side)

ACTIVITY SCUBA or Snorkel

SKILL LEVEL Advanced Diver, good rock climber

DEPTH 70 feet maximum

TRANSPORTATION Car

DIRECTIONS Coming from Kahului, look for a small space to pull off the road just before you make the loop down to Maliko Gulch. Just opposite you'll see where a paved road (Hamakuapoko Rd.) connects to the highway (there's no street sign giving its name, however). Park here and look for the trail down to the right.

WHEN Best in SUMMER.

WHERE TO DIVE Enter on the left or right side of the lava outcropping, whichever is the most protected on that given day. Head straight out and follow your instincts under water. You can also arrive here by swimming across from the right side of Maliko Bay, but you'll have to swim back against the prevailing currents.

WHAT TO EXPECT Gorgeous reef, extremely colorful. Plenty of fish life and good spear fishing. The relief is also good with deep crevasses and underwater mountain ranges. Large ULUA frequent the area along with UHU, A'AWA, KUMU, PUALU, SQUIRREL FISH, VARIOUS SURGEON FISH, and a host of others.

HAZARDS Rough surf can make the entry dangerous and the currents running toward Kahului may give you a ride. Above all, watch the walk down!

FACILITIES Same as most of my dives - zip.

COMMENTS A full wet suit is recommended for the entry. A set of knee pads at least. Snorkelers can head over to the left where it's not so deep. Don't attempt entry here if the seas are large and pounding in on the rocks.

Maliko Bay (Left Side)

The trail down, and entry.

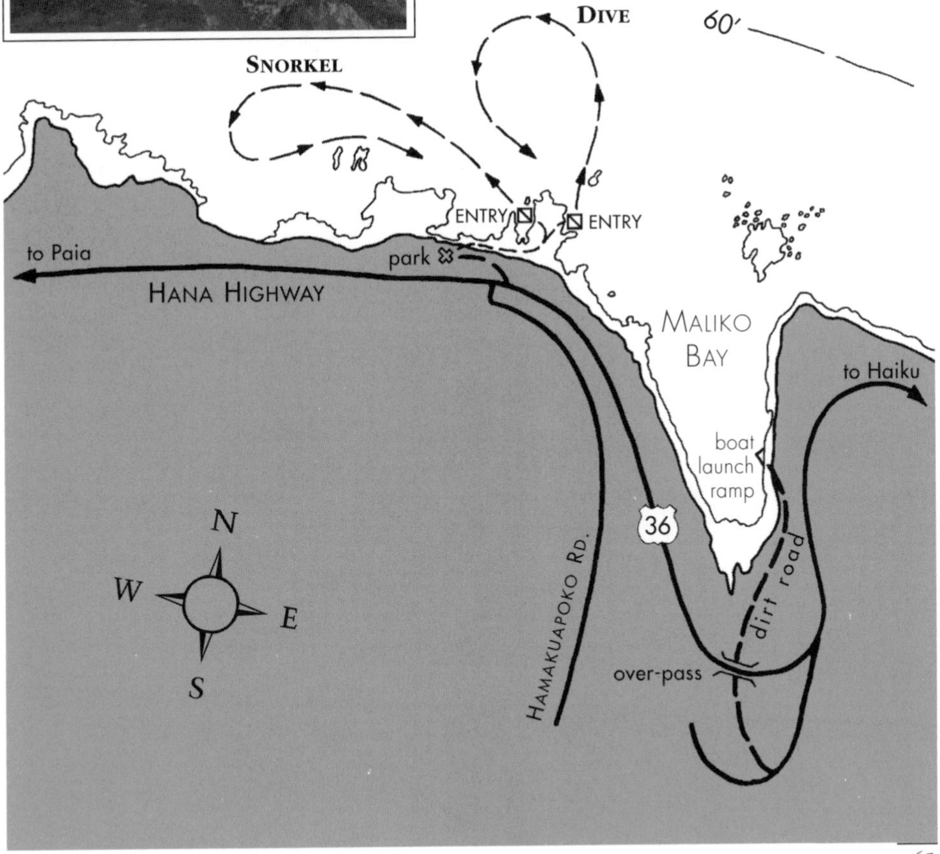

DIVE

SNORKEL

60'

ENTRY

ENTRY

to Paia

HANA HIGHWAY

park

MALIKO BAY

to Haiku

boat launch ramp

N
W   E
S

HAMAKUAPOKO RD.

36

dirt road

over-pass

KAHAKULOA

ACTIVITY   SCUBA

SKILL LEVEL   Advanced Diver, part mountain goat

DEPTH   The reef plays out at 70 feet

TRANSPORTATION   Car

DIRECTIONS   Coming from Wailuku, look for a small space to pull off the side of the road at the 15.7 mile marker. Walk straight down to the ocean from there. It's not much of a trail (fake it).

WHEN   Best in SUMMER or during "Kona weather."

WHERE TO DIVE   Go either left or right once you enter the water. Enter off the right side of the lava flow.

WHAT TO EXPECT   A steep hill and strenuous climb down. Definitely not for the squeamish. The entry is semi-tricky. It's safe enough if the water's not very rough. Many varieties of reef fish are supported by the reef including UKU, ULUA, PAPIO, A'AWA, PO'OU, PUALU, KUMU, and several inedible species. The relief is good and yet the presence of lobster in the area is virtually non-existent. SEA TURTLES are fairly common and jellyfish can be a problem.

HAZARDS   Mainly the walk down, and rough seas making the entry impossible.

FACILITIES   Absolutely nothing.

COMMENTS   Bring a full wet suit or at least knee pads. If the dive doesn't kill you, the walk back will.

This proves it's not impossible.

KAHAKULOA

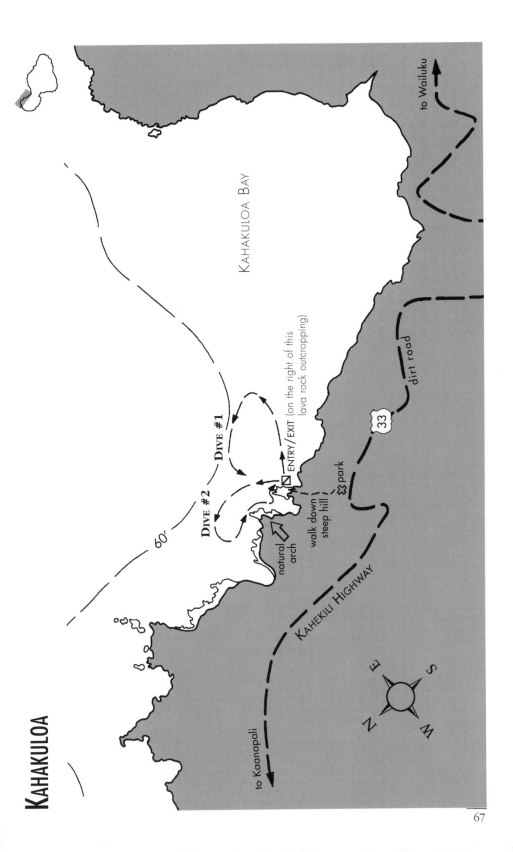

KAHAKULOA BAY

DIVE #1

DIVE #2

60'

ENTRY/EXIT (on the right of this lava rock outcropping)

natural arch

walk down steep hill

park

33

dirt road

to Wailuku

KAHEKILI HIGHWAY

to Kaanapali

N
W — E
S

MOKOLEA POINT

ACTIVITY	SCUBA
SKILL LEVEL	Advanced Diver
DEPTH	The reef hits sand bottom at 110 feet. There's another underwater "mountain" a short ways beyond that.
TRANSPORTATION	Truck or car with good clearance
DIRECTIONS	Coming from Wailuku, look for a dirt road on your right (ocean side) at the 16.2 mile marker. Follow it in and stop just a little short of its end (it's about a block long). From here, make your own trail to the protected cove on your left (as you face the ocean).
WHEN	SUMMER or during periods of KONA WINDS.
WHERE TO DIVE	Once you get out of the small protected cove, head straight out to sea. Circle around to your left and make your way back to the same cove for your exit.
WHAT TO EXPECT	This is one of, if not the BEST, dives on any of Maui's north shore. The variety and abundance of fish life is incredible! The coral is very colorful and forms elaborate and irregular underwater relief out at the 60 to 80 foot deep areas. Deep cuts and crevices make the ideal habitat for large ULUA (blue jacks). It's an excellent area for underwater photography and spear fishing. Lobsters, however, are not too plentiful. The entry in the small cove is fairly well protected during periods of moderate trade winds during the summer, but can be dangerous in rougher water.
HAZARDS	Winter's northwest swell pounds straight into the cove making diving here during the winter seldom possible. Strong trade winds during the summer can cause swells so large that they wrap around and crash into the cove. In either case, the entry and exit can be extremely dangerous! If the water's too rough, try Honanana Bay just a block or so back to the west of Mokolea Point. It's much better protected from summer's strong trade winds.
FACILITIES	Zero.
COMMENTS	A full wet suit is a MUST for protection. It's easy to get lost here. When you surface after your dive is over, all the lava rock coves look alike. Place a bright marker on a high rock pinnacle to mark your exit. You'll be glad you did! Surface a short ways from the rock shoreline, look for the marker, and snorkel in the rest of the way to the exit spot.

MOKOLEA POINT

Enter and exit
from this protected
little cove.

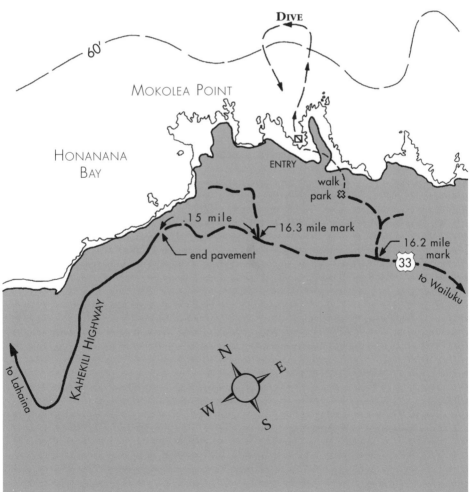

DIVE

60'

MOKOLEA POINT

HONANANA
BAY

ENTRY

walk
park

.15 mile

16.3 mile mark

end pavement

16.2 mile
mark

33

to Wailuku

KAHEKILI HIGHWAY

to Lahaina

N
E
W
S

HONANANA BAY

ACTIVITY   SCUBA

SKILL LEVEL   Intermediate to Advanced Level Divers; Advanced Level mountain goats for the climb down.

DEPTH   50 feet is about the deepest you'll get

TRANSPORTATION   Car with good ground clearance

DIRECTIONS   Coming from Wailuku, turn right on one of the many dirt roads in the area at the 16.33 mile marker. Check your odometer carefully. There are several other dirt roads to confuse you. Head in a short ways and veer to the left. Drive to the edge of the cliff overlooking Honanana Bay. From here head straight north on the foot path down to the water. When you reach the bottom, turn left and wade across a small inlet forming a 2 foot deep tide pool to a lava rock ledge facing a miniature lava rock island. Drop in here and look for the small island to guide yourself back out at the end of your dive.

WHEN   SUMMER is best; sometimes in the FALL.

WHERE TO DIVE   Either straight out to sea or head over to the middle of the bay. The terrain is similar either way and in either case, the further you go, the deeper it gets.

WHAT TO EXPECT   One of the best protected sites from the prevailing trade winds in the area. It's your ace in the hole on the north shore. This entire bay is replete with colorful and irregularly formed coral. Dozens of varieties of fish inhabit the area making the bay excellent for sight-seeing or spear fishing. I won't even attempt to list them all. This is another one of the more spectacular dives on the island. Highly recommended!

HAZARDS   The walk down's not only hard work, but treacherous. Wading across the tide pool to the lava rock ledge is also slippery and dangerous. Swells crash in here all winter. Don't get in if the surf's up.

FACILITIES   Ha!

COMMENTS   Bring your wet suit for protection here. You're crazy if you don't!

Honanana Bay

Overlooking
Honanana Bay.

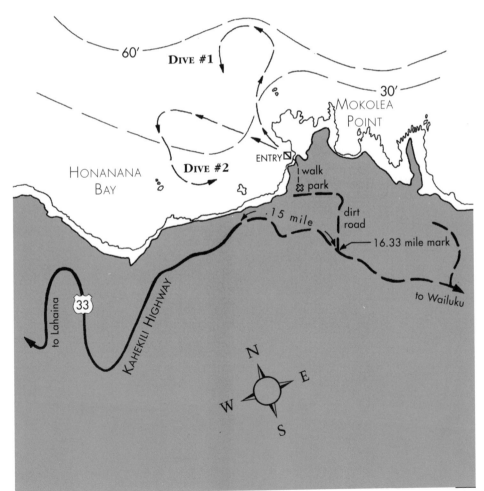

60'

Dive #1

30'

Mokolea Point

Honanana Bay

Dive #2

ENTRY

walk
park

dirt
road

.15 mile

16.33 mile mark

to Wailuku

33

to Lahaina

KAHEKILI HIGHWAY

N
E
W
S

NAKALELE POINT

ACTIVITY	SCUBA
SKILL LEVEL	Advanced Divers (no exceptions)
DEPTH	As deep as 150 feet, but you'll need to remain above 80 feet to make your air last long enough.
TRANSPORTATION	You can get close enough with a car. A jeep will only put you 150 feet closer.
DIRECTIONS	Coming from Lahaina, head north past Honolua Bay until you reach the 38 mile marker. Turn left at the sign for *Nakalele Point Light Station*. Follow the dirt road down a ways, angle to the right, then back again to your left. Try to park as near to the light as you can in whatever you're driving.
WHEN	Best during the SUMMER and AUTUMN; seldom if ever diveable during the winter.
WHERE TO DIVE	Check the map. Head straight out to sea along the wall until you're half out of air. Double back at a different depth so you don't repeat the scenery. The lava flow continues on out underwater well beyond what is visible from above. You can enter in either of two areas. As you face the ocean, walk down to your right for the easiest route down. There is a trail to the left, but the ladder down is unsafe to say the least. You pick.
WHAT TO EXPECT	This is without a doubt one of the most incredible dive sites on the island. It's as close to a wall dive as you'll get anywhere in the state, barring the back side of Molokini Crater. Out from the wall, the bottom drops off quickly to incredible depths with plenty of coral and irregular formations. This is an extremely remote colorful reef area with a full spectrum of marine life. You're likely to see TURTLES, EELS, ULUA, NENUE, PALANI, UHU, PO'OU, PUALU, WEKE, KUMU, A'AWA, SCHOOLS OF BLUE-LINED SNAPPER, HAWK FISH, and many more. This and Mokolea Point are definitely the two best dives on the north side of the West Maui mountains.
HAZARDS	The entry/exit can be extremely dangerous unless the water is really calm.
FACILITIES	This won't take long - zero.
COMMENTS	I'll admit, the hike down is semi-ridiculous. It is worth it though if you can get in. It takes the very best of conditions for this area to be diveable. A full wet suit is a must for protection on the entry/exit. This dive should only be attempted by advanced divers skilled in rough water entries and exits.

Nakalele Point

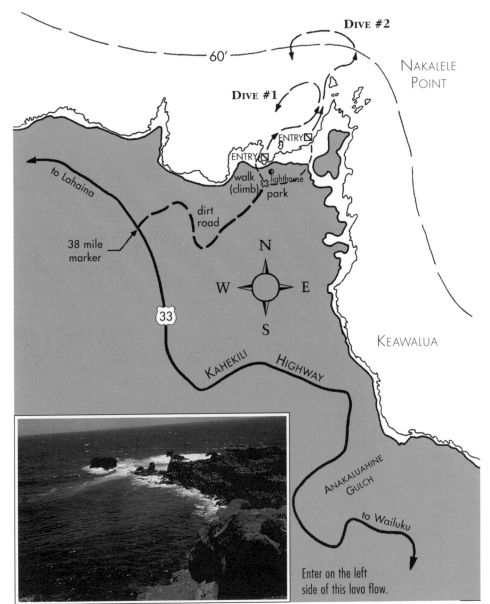

60'

Dive #2

Nakalele Point

Dive #1

ENTRY

ENTRY

walk (climb)

lighthouse

park

to Lahaina

dirt road

38 mile marker

33

N

W   E

S

Kahekili Highway

Keawalua

Anakaluahine Gulch

to Wailuku

Enter on the left
side of this lava flow.

Honokohau Bay

ACTIVITY   SCUBA or Snorkel

SKILL LEVEL   Intermediate Level Divers and Snorkelers

DEPTH   There's no need to go deeper than 50 feet

TRANSPORTATION   Car

DIRECTIONS   Coming from either Lahaina or Wailuku, you'll find Honokohau Bay right at the 36 mile marker. Park right here at the bay.

WHEN   Best in the SUMMER; anytime the bay is calm.

WHERE TO DIVE   Snorkelers...stay to the right, close to the wall. Divers should also head to the right, but not necessarily so close to the wall.

WHAT TO EXPECT   The entry/exit is from a pebble rock beach and the center of the bay is covered by nothing but sand bottom. You'll find a beautiful and colorful reef area over on the right side of the bay with plenty of relief and a good sampling of reef fish – edible and inedible. Spear fishing can be decent. It's just a short walk from the parking area to the entry.

HAZARDS   None when the water is calm.

FACILITIES   A fruit stand across the street.

COMMENTS   This bay is fairly well protected from summer's trade winds and seas built up by them. Very strong winds can cause "wrap-around swells," however. Be sure to watch the surf a while before diving.

Overlooking
Honokohau Bay.

HONOKOHAU BAY

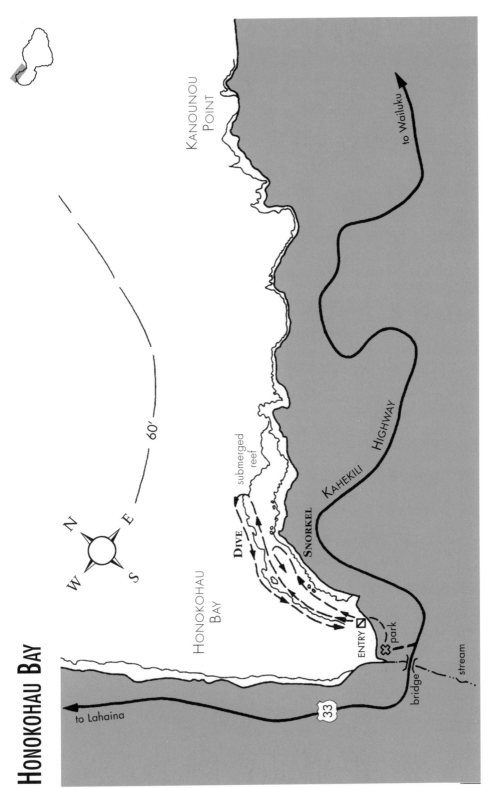

KANOUNOU POINT

to Wailuku

KAHEKILI HIGHWAY

submerged reef

DIVE

SNORKEL

ENTRY

park

HONOKOHAU BAY

60'

N
W E
S

to Lahaina

33

bridge

stream

A Breakdown of Hawaiian Fishes

HAWAIIAN NAME	COMMON NAME	SCIENTIFIC NAME
A'AWA	Black-spot Wrasse Fish	Bodianus Bilunulatus
AHI*	Yellow-Fin Tuna	Thunnus Albacares
AKU*	Skip-Jack Tuna	Katsuwonus Pelamis
ALA'IHI	Jordan's Squirrel Fish	Flammeo Scythrops
ALO'ILO'I	White-spotted Damsel Fish	Dascyllus Albisella
AWA	Milk Fish	Chanos Chanos
AWEOWEO	Meek's Big-eye Fish	Priacanthus Meeki
HINALEA	Ballieu's Wrasse Fish	Thalassoma Ballieue
HINALEA HILU	Black Striped Wrasse	Coris Flavovittata
HUMUHUMUNUKUNUKUAPUA'A	Pig-nosed Trigger Fish	Rhinecanthus Rectangulus
KAHALA	Amber Jack	Seriola Dumerili
KAKU	Great Barracuda	Sphyraena Barracuda
KALA	Unicorn Surgeon	Naso Unicornis
KAWA KAWA*	Wavy-back Skipjack	Euthynnus Affinis
KUMU	Purplish Goat Fish	Parupeneus Porphyreus
LAI	Leather-back Fish	Scombroides Sancti-petri
LAUHAU	Lined Butterfly Fish	Chaetodon Lineolatus
	Lemon-colored Butterfly Fish	Chaetodon Citrinellus
	Spotted Butterfly Fish	Chaetodon Miliaris
MAHIMAHI	Dolphin Fish	Coryphaina Hippurus
MANINI	Sandwich Island Surgeon Fish	Acanthurus Sandvicensis
MANO KIHIKIHI	Common Hammerhead Shark	Sphyrna Zygaena
MANO PA'ELE	Tiger Shark	Galeocerdo Cuvieri
	Black-tipped Reef Shark	Carcharhinus Melanopterus
	White-tipped Reef Shark	Triaenodon Obesus
MOANO	Yellow-tailed Goat Fish	Parupeneus Chryseryduos
MU	Grand-eyed Porgy	Monotaxis Olivaceus
NA'ENA'E	Orange-spot Surgeon Fish	Acanthurus Olivaceus
NENUE	Ash-colored Rudder Fish	Kyphosus Cinerescens
NOHU	Jenkin's Scorpion Fish	Scorpaenopsis Cacopsis
OILI LEPA	Blue-lined Leather Jacket	Osbeckia Scripta
OMILU	Forskal's Jack Fish	Carangoides Ferdau
ONO*	The Wahoo Fish	Acanthocybium Solarndri
O'OPU HUE	Common Porcupine Fish	Diodon Holacanthus

HAWAIIAN NAME	COMMON NAME	SCIENTIFIC NAME
PALANI	Dussumier's Surgeon Fish	Acanthurus Dusumieri
PILIKOA	Forster's Hawk Fish	Paracirrhites Forsteri
PUALU	Ring-tailed Surgeon Fish	Acanthurus Mata
PUALU	Yellow-finned Surgeon Fish	Acanthurus Xanthopterus
PO'OU	Rose-colored Wrasse Fish	Bodianus Bilunulatus
PUHI LAU MILO	Common Moray Eel	Gymnothorax Undulatus
UHU	Red and Violet Parrot Fish	Scarops Rubroviolaceus
UHU ULIULI	Large Blue Parrot Fish	Scarus Perspicillatus
UKU	Blue-green Snapper Fish	Aprion Virescens
	Blue-lined Snapper Fish	Lutjanus Kasmira
ULAE	Variegated Lizard Fish	Synodus Variegatus
ULUA PA'O PA'O	Yellow Jack Fish	Gnathonodon Speciosus
ULUA, BLACK	Black Jack Fish	Caranx Lugubris
ULUA, BLUE	Blue Jack Fish	Caranx Melampygus
ULUA, WHITE	White Jack Fish	Caranx Ignoblis
U'U	Forskal's Squirrel Fish	Myripristis Murdjan
WEKE	Samoan Goat Fish	Mulloikichthys Samoensis
	Argus Grouper	Cephalopholis Argus
	Boar Fish	Histiopterus Typus

* These fish are found in much deeper water and are virtually never sighted by divers. I included them since you might run into them on your menu at the restaurant.

A BRIEF DESCRIPTION OF HAWAIIAN WEATHER PATTERNS AND THEIR EFFECT ON SHORE DIVING

Shore diving poses an entirely different set of considerations for divers than boat diving. On boat dives we generally leave the details of weather to the captain and we concentrate merely on our diving. On shore dives we can no longer sit back and let someone else figure it all out for us. A basic knowledge of Hawaiian weather and its effects is essential. You must know how to interpret the different CURRENTS, WINDS, WAVES, and TIDES in order to choose the proper dive site for a particular day. The advanced diver learns not only how to interpret the weather but how to work with the winds, currents, and swells and incorporate them in his total dive plan.

The biggest problem shore divers face is not in the water or on the land. It's where the two meet! In other words, where the waves pound you into the rocks and grind you on the beach! Most waves are caused by winds, so first let's discuss the different WINDS affecting Hawaii.

TRADE WINDS: The strong and steady winds out of the east and northeast are by far the most predominant weather force in the islands. Winds come from all directions but come from the east at least 70% of the time at an average speed of 12 knots. The Pacific Anticyclone, a high pressure center, is the cause of the trade winds in Hawaii. In the summer, the high pressure system is well developed over the eastern North Pacific and maintains a fairly steady position northeast of the islands. In the winter, the high is weaker and not as consistent. Subsequently, summer's trade winds are much steadier and stronger than are winter's. Don't misunderstand; there are periods of strong trade winds during the winter. They just don't occur on as regular a basis. July has the most consistent trades while January has the least consistent. Trade winds funneling through the channels between the islands pick up speed from their original velocity over open ocean, making these areas particularly hazardous. Only the leeward sides of most of the islands are left protected from the seas built up by strong trade winds. The trades in the Alenuihaha Channel, between Maui and the Big Island, are reported to be the strongest of all channel winds making this one of the most respected and dangerous of all channels for ocean activities! Fishermen venture out here only on the calmest of days and allow plenty of time to get back before the winds pick up. The winds in the Pailolo Channel, between Maui and Molokai, come in a close second with the Kaiwi Channel, between Oahu and Molokai, right behind. However, channel winds of equal velocity build up the highest waves in the Kauai Channel, between Oahu and Kauai, due to the extreme width of the channel. The size of this channel more closely approximates conditions over the open ocean. All said and done, trades over the open ocean funnel into the strongest channel winds and build up the highest waves in the Alenuihaha Channel.

KONA WINDS: Kona winds, usually associated with a low pressure system near the islands, come from the south or southwest and are almost always accompanied by rain and stormy weather. Kona is the Polynesian word for leeward, and describes the direction from whence they come. Periods of Kona winds don't last too long, thankfully. They also build up seas and swells from the southerly direction, churning up the water and making entries on the south side of the islands tough and visibility poor. Kona storms can be very destructive but weaker Kona weather can sometimes have the beneficial effect of counteracting the northwest swell common in the winter and make north shore diving attractive for a short period (if you're on the ball).

HURRICANES: This is definitely not the time to dive, nor afterward. Huge swells built up during hurricanes and tropical storms not only eat the beaches but stir up the water so much that visibility can be zero up to a mile out for as much as a month afterward. If you're coming to Hawaii to dive, you might consider our weather before you hop on the plane.

Next, we need to discuss the WAVES that are caused by all these winds. Basically, winds blowing over water produce waves. The water is not moving laterally as it appears. It's merely moving up and down. Nevertheless, waves soon turn into swells and can make shore entries dangerous if not impossible. The main source of problems in this category for divers is winter's strong northwest swell.

NORTHWEST SWELL: The same swell that warms the hearts of surfers on Oahu, Molokai and Maui sends divers running to the opposite sides of the islands looking for just the opposite - calm seas. There have been several periods during the past ten years when northwest swells have exceeded 25 feet in height (trough to crest).

EASTERLY SWELLS: Almost all year, the trade winds pump in moderately large swells from the east and northeast making that side of all islands hazardous. Divers need to look for periods of extremely light winds (5 to 15 knots) for any hopes of getting in on the windward side of the islands.

SOUTHERLY SWELL: Kona storms, or storms from the southern hemisphere, can produce swells from the south large enough to preclude diving on the south shores of all islands. Periods of south swells are uncommon but are a force to be reckoned with. South shore spots are seldom diveable during these periods. Knowledge of all these conditions can be readily had via the Marine Weather Forecast which I'll discuss later.

TSUNAMI: An open ocean wave generated by an underwater earthquake or volcanic eruption is called a tsunami. They can come from as far as South America or be generated locally. They travel as fast as 500 miles per hour, but can allow several hours warning depending on their point of generation. This is not the case with locally generated ones. In the case of a violent earthquake right here, you should evacuate the beach or water immediately and head for higher ground. Listen for the loud siren (tsunami warning) and be prepared to react. Occurrences have been non-existent recently, but you never know!

Another potential hazard to shore divers is CURRENT. The currents in Hawaiian waters are the result of several factors. First let's discuss the effect of the tides.

TIDES: I'm sure you know that tides are caused by the gravitational pull of the moon on the earth's surface. It's more complicated than that, but basically the moon pulls the water away from the solid earth slightly as it travels around the earth in its orbit. Tides follow the moon as it rotates around the planet. The sun also exerts a pull on the water but is not as noticeable as that of the moon. There are periods of extra high tides when the sun and moon line up about twice each month. The difference between high and low tides in Hawaii is approximately 2 feet. As the tides rise and drop they cause the water to move through the islands. At high tide the water moves toward the south southwest and vice-versa during periods of low tide. High tides are called flood tides and low tides are called ebb tides. Currents caused by tides seem to be the most serious threat to shore divers. Strong running tidal currents can be fast enough to outpace your rate of surface swimming with full SCUBA gear. If you're out of air and forced to swim on the surface against it, you may not be able to make any headway. Serious situations may call for the ditching of your weight belt or even your tank. The water may even be running one direction on the surface and the opposite underneath. Be prepared to adjust your dive plan after you submerge and see which direction the water is really running. A little forethought can help eliminate the need for drastic measures. Whenever possible, head into the current on the way out and swim back to your exit point with the current.

OCEANIC AND TRADE WIND DRIVEN CURRENTS: Both oceanic currents and those driven by the trades run toward the west and average .5 to 1 knot in velocity. I'll admit, this is only a generalization. In reality, they swirl around the islands and create a somewhat more confused picture. They're not usually as strong as the tidal currents and are much more predictable. Consequently, they pose less of a problem to shore divers. In the case of real emergency, one can always pull him/herself along the bottom against strong currents. Grab something solid but try to avoid coral, since coral polyps are very fragile and are crushed easily by the diver's gloved hand.

Now for a brief mention of –

HAWAII'S WATER TEMPERATURE: In the islands, water temperatures range from the upper 60's to the lower 80's. A full 2 mm or 1/8" body glove type wet suit is recommended if you're going to make repetitive dives. Of course, this varies with the person's fat content in his or her body. A 3/16" short-sleeve top is commonly used for boat diving in the islands. A full wet suit offers protection not only from the cold but from the sharp lava rock fronting much of the state's coastline. The water is coldest in January and February and warmest in August and September.

Finally, to find out what the prevailing weather conditions in the various islands are you need to utilize the services of the –

NATIONAL WEATHER SERVICE: The National Weather Service issues marine weather forecasts for all the islands and updates them several times during the day. The forecasts may be obtained by listening to various radio broadcasts or by phoning these numbers on each island for a recorded message:

| Maui ....877-3477 | Molokai ....552-2477 | Lanai............565-6033 |
| Oahu ....836-3921 | Hawaii..........935-9883 | Kauai...........245-3569 |

Ideal conditions exist when the forecast calls for light and variable trade winds 5 to 15 mph and seas 2 to 4 feet in the coastal areas and 4 to 8 feet in the channels. Seas of 8 to 12 feet are becoming too large for safe entries unless you know of certain "protected areas." Use these phone numbers continuously to keep yourself on top of the entire weather picture during your stay and plan your dives accordingly.

Chuck Thorne